Taco!
Taco!
Taco!

Over 100 Recipes for Everybody

SARA HAAS
FOREWORD BY Bryan Roof

hatherleigh

Hatherleigh Press is committed to preserving and protecting
the natural resources of the earth. Environmentally
responsible and sustainable practices are embraced
within the company's mission statement.

Visit us at www.hatherleighpress.com and register online
for free offers, discounts, special events, and more.

Taco! Taco! Taco!

Text copyright © 2018 Sara Haas

Library of Congress Cataloging-in-Publication Data
is available upon request.

ISBN: 978-1-57826-752-1

COVER AND INTERIOR DESIGN BY CAROLYN KASPER

Printed in the United States

10 9 8 7 6 5 4 3 2 1

For my loving and patient husband,
my adorable sous chef, and my beyond
supportive friends, family, and colleagues.
And for our little Lucy, you will
always be in our hearts.

Contents

THE RECIPES

Foreword

THE SIMPLEST FOODS ARE often the hardest to perfect because there's very little to hide behind. A taco is such a food. I would argue a good taco is 75 percent the quality of the tortilla, be it corn or flour; 20 percent filling—the guisado, carne asada, grilled vegetable medley, or tofu pup, if that's your thing; and 5 percent garnish, the stuff that carries it over the edge—a squeeze of lime, a sprinkling of chopped onion and cilantro, salsa, your sriracha-crema (for the hipsters in the crowd). One foul element can throw your taco into a tailspin of mediocrity.

I'm a taco purist. If presented with a bevy of filling options, I'll always opt for carnitas—chunks of pork, usually from the shoulder, cooked in lard until slightly crisp and fall-apart tender. A good quality corn tortilla, which is often harder to find than good carnitas, makes all the difference. For garnish, just a sprinkling of minced onion and cilantro, maybe a squeeze of lime. I don't even consider salsa until I'm on my third or fourth taco. Much like a Texas pitmaster believes that good barbecue doesn't need sauce, a good filling and tortilla should stand on their own.

I've come a long way to be this stuck up about my tacos. Like Sara, I grew up on ground beef tacos, seasoned with a spice packet and cooked up slightly soupy, all folded into a microwaved flour tortilla that was as sure as your heartburn to spring a leak. And there were garnishes: shredded iceberg lettuce, diced tomato, pre-shredded cheese with its light coating of cornstarch that gave it the illusion of freshness beyond its days, and maybe some of those minced onions that I still love. On a rare occasion, there were hard taco shells, which I never quite understood.

This clever book serves as a lucid reminder that experimentation, not pre-packaged taco seasoning, is really the spice of life. Tacos, perhaps more than any other food, lend themselves to variety. After all, there's more to a taco than tradition. I'm glad that Sara has given license to the home cook to take shortcuts, streamline the process, invent new flavor combinations, and to get into the kitchen and play. Because ultimately, it's all about shoving tacos in your face.

Bryan Roof
Executive Food Editor for Cook's Country *by America's Test Kitchen*

Introduction

YOU LOVE TACOS, RIGHT? I'm pretty sure that's why you bought this book. Here's the great news—I love tacos too. It seems so crazy to write a book all about tacos, but that's just what I decided to do. Let me give you a little back story on my taco obsession.

My favorite meal as a kid (besides my mom's famous chicken and noodles and chili) was tacos! They were the kind you make from a box, but hey, they were good and I thought it was so much fun "building" my own.

As years passed by, I continually found myself drawn to those tacos. I loved how easily they came together and I loved all of the flavors. Imagine my surprise, many years later, when I discovered those flavors *aren't* the only flavors you can use for tacos. The world opened up and tacos became an even bigger obsession!

I found out about fish tacos, chiles, pico de gallo, carne asada, and guacamole! It was all so magical. Every place I went or vacationed, I made sure to find a restaurant that specialized in tacos. And each time, I was so amazed at how different they could be.

I started thinking—"aren't tacos pretty perfect?" I mean, you can basically take any food and put it in a tortilla and it can be amazing. The possibilities of combinations are endless. Then, I thought, "wouldn't it be fun to write a cookbook about these possibilities?" Why not teach *everyone* about the marvel that is the taco. And why not teach them not to limit themselves when it comes to what's inside of those tacos.

I'm a dietitian. Maybe that makes you happy? Or maybe that makes you cringe? I hope it makes you happy, but if it did make you raise your eyebrows, let me clarify some things for you. Dietitians are not your enemies, we are your friends. We care about your health, that's all. We make your life easier by translating science so that you can make the best, most nutritious decisions for you! See, we're awesome! But here's the deal: I'm not writing this book to teach you about nutrition. I'm writing this book sans calorie or nutrition information. Why? Because that's not how I roll.

Nope. Instead, I like to make reasonably-sized food that uses delicious, mostly nutritious ingredients that taste good.

With that in mind, most importantly, I want you to have fun! Get in the kitchen with your friends and family or some good music and a glass of wine and get dirty. Make a mess. *Just have fun*! And at the end, you'll be rewarded with the ultimate gift—tacos!

Chapter 1

HOW TO USE THIS BOOK

HOORAY, NO RULES!

Here's the deal with this book: there are no rules! Seriously, just pick a recipe that sounds good and make it. You'll see plenty of tips and tricks along the way to help you. Some recipes require more ingredients and perhaps a little more work, but I promise, I don't make anything difficult. And your effort is always rewarded at the end with a delicious taco!

BUT I *NEED* RULES!

I know some of you will require rules, and I respect that. So, for you, I've outlined a few things in the front section of this book to give you some guidance. Note that all of these are kind suggestions, designed to give you more confidence in the kitchen. Hopefully they help you make more informed choices at the store or instill some sense of excitement when it comes to cooking. If that happens, then I have been successful!

HAVE FUN!

I may have lied when I said there are no rules to this book. There are actually two rules you must follow: the first is to have fun! If at any point you are not having fun, put the book down and walk away. Come back when you're ready. It'll be waiting for you (I'm sure it won't come to this, though, because these recipes aren't designed to frustrate you. They're designed for you to have fun in your kitchen). The second rule is to *read* the recipe first. Yes, sounds like I'm being a bit obnoxious by saying that, but really, read the whole recipe before you get started. That way there won't be any surprises along the way. This also makes Rule #1, to have fun, easier!

TACO TIME

On to a few details. This book is all about tacos, but these aren't "normal" tacos. That means normal taco rules don't apply. I like to think of all recipes merely as suggestions, or starting points, letting my imagination fill in the blanks or point me somewhere else. I want you to feel the same way. Don't feel limited by what I present here. For example, if you see cabbage listed as an ingredient in the recipe, don't feel like you have to use it. I mean, I love cabbage (as you'll soon find out), but if it's not your thing, don't sweat it! Instead, swap in something else to replace it. Not sure what that swap is? I'll try to help you along the way, but I also encourage you to come up with ideas, too! You're smart; you bought this book, right?

Chapter 2

GROCERY TIPS

GROCERIES 101:
THE 3-STEP PLAN

Lᴇᴛ's ᴛᴀʟᴋ ɢʀᴏᴄᴇʀɪᴇꜱ—ꜱᴘᴇᴄɪꜰɪᴄᴀʟʟʏ, ᴛʜᴇ grocery *store* and your relationship with it. For many of us, shopping at the grocery store is a necessary evil. Let's face it; we don't love making grocery lists, we don't love maneuvering the grocery cart down those big aisles that always seem so crowded, and we always end up spending more money and time there than we mean to. Is there a way to make the whole experience of planning, buying, and putting away groceries more enjoyable, while also saving you time and money? Well of course there is, and that's what this chapter is all about!

STEP 1:
SET UP A WINNING GROCERY LIST

Going to the grocery store is kind of like making it to "the big game" in sports. You don't just show up to the game unprepared and untrained, right? You have to practice and prepare—get mentally and physically ready for anything and everything. Same goes for that trip to the store. You know what happens when you wander in without a game plan—lost time and money. To prevent that, you need to lay some groundwork and come up with a game plan. Part of that plan is making a successful grocery list. How do you do that? First, pick your platform: your phone, a piece of paper, whatever is easiest and simplest for you. Next, grab your recipes. Then—and this is the most important part—when you make your list, divide it into sections based on how your grocery store is laid out. So, if the produce section is first, make that the first section on your list. Then continue the sections that way, so that you can start at one end and finish at the other. Now it's all about filling up those sections with the foods you need. That's it! And while you're at it, you may want to consider purchasing your refrigerated and frozen foods at the end of the shopping trip. These are perishable foods and need to stay cold. If you pick them up last, you decrease the odds of their thawing and spoiling in your cart while you're shopping.

STEP 2:
YOU'RE AT THE STORE, NOW WHAT?

It's a distracting place, that grocery store. With free samples, delicious smells, and packages of eye-catching goodies everywhere, it's easy to waste your day and money away in there. But, you've got to stick to your game plan, and that means sticking to that grocery list. Besides being distracted at the store, sometimes you may find yourself struggling with picking out the right produce or meat. Standing in front of the cucumbers and staring at them certainly isn't a winning way to choose the best one. I get it—that's why I put together a complete guide (starting on page 8) to help you navigate the grocery store like a pro. This handy guide is designed to help you pick out the freshest and best foods.

STEP 3:
YOU'RE AT HOME, NOW WHAT?

Congratulations! You went to the store, got just what you needed, and it didn't take that long or cost as much as it usually does! Yahoo! All of your groceries are now safely home, but now what? Of course, you know where things go, or do you? You might be surprised by where foods are best stored so that they maintain freshness—or, in the case of raw meat, poultry, and fish, where they go so that they won't cross-contaminate other food. Use this food storage guide to help you put your groceries away in the right places.

FOOD STORAGE GUIDE

Main Compartment:

Milk and other dairy
(keep towards the back)

Cooked food, including
cooked meat and leftovers

Bottom Shelf:

Eggs (keep in the carton)

Raw meat, poultry, fish, and
seafood (best if kept in a
bowl or plastic bag)

Crisper Bins:

Keep your produce here;
hopefully you have two,
one for fruits and one
for vegetables

The Door:

Condiments

NAVIGATE THE GROCERY STORE LIKE A PRO

How many times have you been at the grocery store and felt frustrated because you weren't sure if that melon was ripe or if you were getting the freshest eggs? The grocery store can be a confusing place, but with a few tips, you'll be able to navigate it like a pro! Not only will this save you time and money, but also prevent food waste.

The Produce Section

AVOCADOS: Ripe avocados should give with slight pressure and be free from soft spots and deep bruises. They can be purchased firm—just leave them out on the counter to ripen, which should take a few days at room temperature. Speed up the process by placing them in a paper bag.

PINEAPPLE: A ripe pineapple should be heavy for its size, mostly yellow in color, with little, if any, green. It should be fragrant, smelling of pineapple. If overly brown or soft, it's likely over-ripe. You can test ripeness by pulling at an inner leaf on the top. If it comes out easily, it's ripe. If it doesn't, it's not ripe.

MELON: Like pineapple, it should be heavy for its size. It should be firm, without dents or bruises. For cantaloupe, the color under its brown netting should be mostly orange or tan, and when you press on the area where the melon was once attached to the vine, it should be soft. On watermelon, look for a large yellow spot on the belly, which means it ripened while sitting in the sun. A white or green belly means the melon was harvested too soon and may not be ripe. Watermelon should be heavy for its size and if knocked, it should sound dull and hollow.

MANGO: Ripe mangos are soft, but not mushy to the touch. Avoid overly softened mangos or mangos with dark spots, which may indicate it's overly ripe and going bad. Unripe mangos can be placed in a paper bag at room temperature to speed up ripening. Ripe mangos can be stored in the refrigerator.

BERRIES: Do your best to look berries over and don't purchase if you see any signs of mold or "furry stuff." Berries should be brightly colored and slightly firm, free of bruises and mushy spots. Once home, don't wash berries immediately unless you plan on eating them. Water may cause them to start getting moldy faster. Transfer berries to a breathable container (such as a colander) and store in the main compartment of your refrigerator.

CHERRIES: Fresh cherries should be bright red, shiny, firm to the touch, and show no signs of bruising or soft spots. Stems should be intact so that they last longer. Keep unwashed in a bag in the refrigerator.

PEACHES: Firm peaches will ripen on the counter. Ripe peaches should give slightly to the touch and be free from bruises and soft spots. Place in a paper bag, with a few holes for venting, to ripen at room temperature. Add an apple to speed up the process. Store ripened peaches in the fridge.

TOMATOES: Ripe tomatoes are heavy for their size, are brightly colored, and give slightly when touched. Avoid any with bruises or signs of broken skin. Keep on the counter at room temperature and not in the refrigerator. Place in a paper bag, with a few holes for venting, to ripen at room temperature. Add an apple to speed up the process.

BRUSSELS SPROUTS: Look for small sprouts that are tightly wrapped. Avoid those that appear "opened" or that have any sign of molding or discoloration. Store unwashed in the refrigerator.

GARLIC: Garlic heads should be tightly closed, not revealing any of their cloves. They should have no soft spots, and whole heads should be stored in a dark, cool place.

ONIONS: Choose onions that are still wrapped in their papery skin. Avoid ones with soft spots, signs of mold, or dents. Store in a cool, dark place.

POTATOES: Choose potatoes that are firm to the touch, and don't have blemishes, wrinkles, or soft spots, or are overly green. Keep in a dark, dry, cool place with good ventilation. The pantry is the perfect spot!

PRE-PACKAGED PRODUCE: Look at contents and use your best judgment. Lettuce should look crisp, not wilted or brown. Broccoli and other veggies should be firm and not have brown spots. Always refer to the "best by" date on the package. Choose one that has a date furthest from the day you buy it—that means it's the freshest of the bunch. Don't be afraid to reach to the back of the case to find it!

GENERAL PRODUCE INFO

PRODUCE DRAWERS: Use those produce drawers! They're made specifically to house your favorite perishables. And heed their advice of keeping the veggies and fruit separate. They require different humidity levels, which, if you follow, will help keep your produce fresher for longer.

GENERAL: Pre-packaged produce versus free-standing produce, is there a difference? Not necessarily, especially nutritionally speaking, one is just more convenient (sometimes) than the other. It's really a matter of preference. The bagged stuff saves some time because it's usually washed, cut, and ready to go. Whereas if you buy the produce in its whole state, you'll have to spend a little extra time in the kitchen prepping it. The time savings is passed along at a cost to you, as those pre-packaged goodies will likely cost more than their whole counterparts. And be sure to read labels on those pre-cut veggies and fruit—sometimes they aren't washed, which means you'll have to do that before you use them in any of your cooking.

The Dairy Aisle

COW'S MILK: Always refer to the "sell by" date on the container. Choose the one with the date furthest in the future. Store in fridge, in the main compartment, not in the door. For the recipes in this book, any type of milk will work. A milk that is higher in fat content (2% or whole milk) will sometimes help with adding richness to a dish, especially in the Dessert recipes, but lower-fat milk and even milk alternatives will still work.

EGGS: Refer to the package numbers; they include the plant date, the packaging date, and the sell by date. The plant number is first, followed by the packaging date, written as a 3 digit number, reflecting the day of the year. For example, January 1 would be "001." Typically fresh eggs, if stored properly, will be good up to five weeks past this date. Buy eggs before their "sell by" date (the last date the store is able to sell the eggs) and store in the main compartment of your refrigerator in their original carton.

YOGURT: Always refer to the "sell-by" date on the container. Choose the one with the date furthest in the future. Store in fridge, in the main compartment, not in the door. Buy plain versions and flavor yourself to avoid added sugar. Or look for a brand that has very little added sugar.

The Grains

CEREALS: Choose 100% whole grain cereals, which are often identified on the label, or look at the ingredient list to be sure a whole grain is listed somewhere near the beginning. For example, whole wheat flour, whole grain oat flour, et cetera. Look for cereals that have at least 3 to 5 grams of fiber per serving and less than 8 grams of sugar per serving (less is always better, though, when it comes to sugar)!

BREAD: Choose 100% whole grain varieties and opt for ones that don't have a million ingredients. The whole grain should be the first ingredient listed. Bread slices should be about 1 ounce and should contain about 80 to 100 calories, at least 2 grams of fiber, and less than 200 milligrams of sodium.

GENERIC VERSUS BRAND: Generic can be just as good as brand names. Simply take a few extra minutes to compare labels. You might find the ingredient lists are identical or virtually identical. If that's the case, go with the generic, as it's typically less expensive!

BULK VERSUS BOXED: Buying in bulk can make a lot of sense, especially if you're feeding a crowd or following a budget. Just be sure that the bulk turnover is pretty good (meaning that the bins are replenished often so that you're getting the freshest ingredients). When in doubt, go with the boxed versions, especially if you or a family member has a food allergy. Both are equally nutritious, so it's a matter of preference.

The Meat and Fish Department

If you're not sure about something in the meat department, your butcher is an amazing resource. No butcher? Talk to the person who's in charge of stocking the meat section at your store.

Here are some good questions to ask:

- How fresh is this meat/poultry/fish? When was it brought in to the store?
- Was this meat/poultry/fish previously frozen? If so, how long is it good for?
- If meat is frozen, what is the best way to thaw it?
- For ground meat and poultry, when was it ground? How many days do I have to consume it?
- For big cuts or whole pieces (such as whole chicken), can you trim or break down into pieces?
- For anything: What are some easy ways to prepare this? Can a less expensive ingredient be substituted?

Finally, for when you get home: Store fresh meat, poultry, and fish, if raw, on the bottom shelf in the fridge. Bonus points for keeping them in a container with sides to catch any potential drips. If the meat is cooked, store in the main compartment of the fridge.

Dates on Packaging

You'll notice that any and all meat you buy will feature a number of dates on the packaging. These dates are mandated by the USDA and provide you with a way to gauge the meat's freshness and quality.

These dates include:

BEST BEFORE DATE: This indicates when a product will be of best flavor or quality. It is *not* a purchase or safety date; it is a freshness date. You should expect the best flavor from the food up to the date listed.

USE BY DATE: This is the last date recommended for use of the product while at peak quality. However, it is *not* a safety date, except when used on infant formula.

SELL BY DATE: This date tells the *store* how long to display the product for sale, and is really for inventory management purposes. It is also *not* a safety date. So, in other words, this date is a communication from the company to the store about how long their product should be for sale. Most foods can last up to a week past this date, but once it hits your home refrigerator, if it's meat, poultry, or fish, it should be cooked in 1–2 days.

Chapter 3

STOCK UP

FILLING THE PANTRY

AS A DIETITIAN AND CHEF, I have learned that people love knowing what things are "must haves" in my kitchen. It's actually one of my favorite questions. But I do find that it changes from time to time. So, for that reason, I'm not only telling you my "Must Haves," but also my "Nice to Haves." The must haves are really kitchen staples, things that I cannot live without. The "Nice to Haves" are things I also like to have, but can still cook without.

Must Haves

Extra-virgin olive oil

Vegetable or canola oil

Balsamic vinegar

Red wine vinegar

White (distilled) vinegar

Kosher salt

Freshly ground black pepper

An array of dried herbs and spices, such as cumin, oregano, chili powder, thyme, cinnamon, red pepper flakes, etc.)

Yellow mustard

Dijon mustard

Honey

Soy sauce

Canned and dry beans

Rolled or steel cut oats

All-purpose flour

White whole wheat flour

Brown and white sugar

Baking soda, baking powder

Vanilla extract

Plain Greek yogurt

Eggs

Milk

Onions of all kinds

Fresh garlic

An array of veggies, such as carrots, bell peppers, tomatoes, lettuce (I love arugula, spinach and romaine)

An array of fruit, such as bananas, apples, lemons, limes, oranges

Whole grain breads, pastas and tortillas

Whole grains (quinoa, bulgur, amaranth, brown rice, etc.)

Nice to Haves

Fresh herbs (cilantro, parsley, thyme)

Finishing oils (almond oil, walnut oil, avocado oil)

Avocados

Vinegars (champagne, rice wine)

Tahini

Miso

Tomato paste

Spices (curry powder, Chinese 5 spice, nutmeg, allspice)

Lentils

Broth, including vegetable, chicken and beef

Frozen or canned fruits and (salt-free) vegetables

Salsa

THE KITCHEN TOOLBOX

Of course, there are items that I must have in my kitchen, and I've listed them here. It's likely you already have some of these items. If you don't have the others, you may want to consider investing in them. These are literally my go-to tools, which means I'm using them all the time. And for these recipes, you'll see that they come in handy. As for the "Nice to Have" items, that's just what they are—nice to have. They can make life easier and are fun to have, but you can live without them.

Must Haves

Chef's knife

Paring knife

2–3 cutting boards of different sizes

Cast iron pan (at least 12 inches)

Wooden spoons

Spatulas (1 big, 1 small, 1 firm and
    1 really pliable)

Whisk

Set of mixing bowls

Measuring cups and spoons

Slow cooker

Blender

Rasp

Juicer (hand held)

Set of stainless steel pans

Grater

Nice to Haves

Pressure cooker

Food processor

Griddle

Grill or grill pan

Stand mixer

Chapter 4

COOKING TIPS AND TRICKS

I KNOW THAT COOKING ISN'T enjoyable for everyone. And that's okay. I understand. Besides not having enough time, maybe you just aren't confident in what you're doing. I get that too. But cooking is like everything else, you have to practice. By practicing, you get better, which equates to confidence.

To help you build that confidence, I'll be offering cooking and recipe tips in the recipes. These little snippets are designed to take away some of the frustration and give you the information you need to succeed in completing a recipe. Besides those tips inside the recipes, I'm offering a few tips here, too. Read them now, and feel free to come back and reference them if you start getting frustrated or overwhelmed!

YOUR KNIFE

Yes, it's time to get your knife out! You're going to put it to good use for these recipes. If you don't have a really great chef's knife, now is the time to treat yourself. You don't have to break the bank, just get yourself a good one and keep it sharp. That means honing it between uses and sharpening it whenever the edge becomes blunt. This not only makes cutting easier for you, it also keeps you safe, because a dull knife is a dangerous knife.

The size and heft of the knife are all a matter of preference. There are millions (well, maybe not millions, but you get what I mean) of types of chef's knives out there. I recommend going to a few stores and trying them out. See how they feel in your hand. If the store will let you chop some stuff with it, do it. There's no better way to "test drive" a knife than using it!

Now that you have your knife, you should know a little about it. Consider this a little crash course on knife skills. First, it's nice to know the anatomy of a knife. Take a look at the photo below and get yourself acquainted.

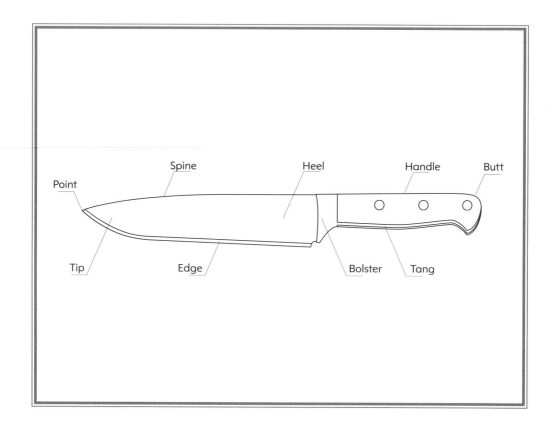

Parts of a Knife

Here's what you need to know about your chef's knife: your grip matters. It seems natural to want to hold the knife right on the handle. However, in order to get the most control on your awesome chef's knife, you'll need to grip it a bit closer to the heel of the blade. The best way to accomplish this is by placing your forefinger and thumb on either side of the bolster and then gripping the handle with your remaining fingers. See the image below.

Now that you know how to hold the knife, you'll also need to practice how to use it. I know, it's really just like anything else. Practice makes perfect! The more you chop, slice, and dice, the better you'll get. Pretty soon you'll be cutting up food like a professional chef, I promise!

When it comes to using the knife, it's all about the rocking motion. You can work more efficiently this way. Your goal, for the most part, is to keep some part of your blade on the cutting board. Say you're cutting a carrot into small cubes. Start with the tip of your blade on the board, then rock the knife back down to the board, ending around the heel of your blade. And just keep doing that, pushing the food towards your knife with your other hand.

Speaking of that other hand, you'll need to protect it! Specifically, you'll need to protect those fingers! The best way to accomplish that is to use what we call "the claw." See the image below:

Holding food this way ensures you won't be slicing more than your food! Essentially, you grip the food with curled fingers and a tucked in thumb. Your knuckles will be gripping the food. Sounds complicated, but again, with practice, you'll be a pro in no time.

And let's not forget about the cutting board! The choice here, again, is really yours. I love a good, heavy wooden board. These hold up well and can take a beating, as long as you take care of them. Remember to use hot, soapy water to clean them and then oil them or maintain them based on the manufacturer's recommendations. If your board cracks or gets a big slice in it, it's time to toss it. Those cracks and slices are breeding grounds for bacteria, so it's not worth the risk. As for plastic, it works just fine and the same rules apply.

No matter what board you choose, be sure to set it up correctly. That's right; did you know there's a way to set up your cutting board? I didn't either, until I went to culinary school, but it makes perfect sense. First, you'll need a few sheets of damp paper towel or a damp thin tea towel. Place that on your work surface, close to the edge, then place your cutting board on top of that.

The damp towel helps keep your board from moving when you're chopping. That's awesome because you'll be using that chef's knife and you don't need a shifting board making your life more challenging. Also, I mentioned that you'll want that towel at the edge of the work surface, and that's true of the board, too. That makes it easier for you to reach the food and use the knife, so no more setting up your cutting board six inches away from you, okay?

KNIFE CUTS

Now that you're all set up and super skilled with holding your knife, you'll need to know what to do with it. Don't fret, I'm here for you! I've included some of my favorite knife cuts here for you to get to know. Some of them are in the book, and some aren't. I figured you might be an over-achiever, so I'm presenting most of them here! And just so you know, the goal is getting the food cut to about the same size so that it all cooks at the same time. Please don't bust out your ruler to measure every cut you make!

ESSENTIAL KNIFE CUTS

KNIFE CUT	SIZE/SHAPE
Chop (rough)	Cuts of about the same size, usually imprecise and irregularly-shaped; pieces are large.
Chop (small)	Cuts of about the same size, usually imprecise and irregularly-shaped; pieces are small
Mince	A very fine chop
Slice	Cuts of the same size, usually in thin pieces
Chiffonade	Fine slices; slices cut into thin ribbons
Zest	A grating away of the outer skin of citrus fruits
Dice, large	¾ inch x ¾ inch x ¾ inch cubes
Dice, medium	½ inch x ½ inch x ½ inch cubes
Dice, small	¼ inch x ¼ inch x ¼ inch cubes
Julienne	⅛ inch x ⅛ inch x 1–2 inches

COOKING MEASUREMENTS

I realize that some of you prob-
ably know this already, but it's
always nice to have a reminder
when it comes to common
household measurements.
So I've included a chart here
for reference.

1 teaspoon	⅓ tablespoon	¼ fluid ounce
3 teaspoons	1 tablespoon	½ fluid ounce
2 tablespoons	⅛ cup	1 fluid ounce
4 tablespoons	¼ cup	2 fluid ounces
8 tablespoons	½ cup	4 fluid ounces
16 tablespoons	1 cup	8 fluid ounces
2 cups	1 pint	16 fluid ounces

COOKING TERMS

If you're new to cooking, you may find some of the words used in recipes confusing. Because of that, I've decided to explain them here, in the front of the book. That way you can reference them at any point when you're cooking. I've only included the methods used in this book. There are more, but that's for another time!

Moist Heat Cooking Methods

Moist heat methods imply you're cooking a food by immersing it in liquid.

BOILING: You know this one: think of boiling water. Boiling means you're cooking a liquid at a temperature of at least 212°F: the liquid is bubbling aggressively.

SIMMER: Simmering happens at a lower temperature, between 185°F-205°F, and involves liquid that is gently bubbling, but not a full, rolling boil.

Dry Heat Methods

Dry heat methods imply you're using a heat source (above or below) to cook them.

ROAST: Done in the oven with the heat source below, the hot air circulates around the food to cook it. Unlike baking, it implies cooking at a higher temperature.

BAKE: Also done with oven with heat source below, allowing the hot air to circulate around the food to cook it. It implies a lower temperature than roasting.

BROIL: This method implies that the heat source is above the food (instead of below); typically the heat is high, allowing the food to cook quickly.

GRILL: The heat source comes from below. That heat source can be charcoal, gas, or electric. Method can be replicated using a grill pan or indoor grill.

Dry Heat Methods (With Fat)

SAUTÉ: In French, sauté means "jump," which somewhat accurately describes this cooking method. Food is cooked in a pan in a small amount of fat over moderate heat. Food is in motion, or "jumping."

SWEAT: Food is cooked in a small amount of fat over a lower heat than what is used for sautéing. This method involves cooking food in order to release some of its moisture.

STIR FRY: Similar to sautéing, but at a much higher heat. Food is cooked quickly this way, typically in a small amount of fat. This method allows small cuts of meat to cook fast and helps keep veggies crisp.

COOKING TEMPERATURES

How many times have you cooked something and wondered, "Is it done yet?" It can be hard to tell by just looking at food to know if it's done. My advice is to invest in a meat thermometer. Yes, spend six to twelve dollars so that you can feel confident about the "doneness" of your food. Checking the temperature of your food is super easy and only takes a few seconds! Here are some tips along with cooking temperatures.

TIP 1: Be sure your thermometer is calibrated so that your reading is accurate. To see if your thermometer is calibrated, you can use one of these two methods. First method: ice water. Fill a glass with ice and then top it off with some water. Let it sit a few minutes, then stick your thermometer in the ice water. It should register at 32°F. If it doesn't, make a small turn on the nut that holds the "stick" part of thermometer to the face of the thermometer. Test again, adjusting as needed. The second method is similar to the first method, but involves boiling water. Set a pot of water over high heat and bring to a boil. Once boiling, insert the thermometer; it should read 212°F. If not, make adjustments as recommended above.

TIP 2: Stick the probe of the thermometer into the thickest part of the food, avoiding any bone. This will let you know if the innermost portion of the food is safely cooked. With that said, it's also important to make sure you insert the thermometer deep enough into the food. Many thermometers bear a little mark or indentation that identifies how far you should insert the probe to get an accurate reading. This is helpful for big things such as roasts and small things, such as meatballs (you may have to skewer two together) or thin cuts of fish or meat.

Now, regarding those temperatures: First things first, while I love a runny egg and a medium-rare steak, there can be some food safety issues with undercooked food. The temperatures below are pulled directly from the USDA and are what I recommend to anyone looking to cook their food safely.

PROTEIN	TEMPERATURE
Ground beef, pork, veal, lamb	160°F
Ground turkey, chicken	165°F
Fresh beef, pork, veal, and lamb (steaks, roasts, and chops)	145°F
Ham, fresh (raw) or "cook before eating"	145°F
Ham, pre-cooked (to reheat)	140°F
Chicken, turkey, duck, and goose (whole or pieces)	165°F
Poultry breast, roasts	165°F
Eggs	Cook yolk and white until firm
Egg dishes	160°F
Egg leftovers and casseroles	165°F

Taken from the USDA

Besides a meat thermometer, I also recommend investing in a refrigerator and freezer thermometer. Many refrigerators come with these already, but I still recommend getting one. They're an inexpensive way to ensure your food stays safe. Be sure to place the thermometer upright, towards the back of your fridge. Check it when you open your fridge to be sure it's staying at or below 40°F. As for your freezer, that thermometer should read 0°F.

GENERAL TIPS

1. **Read the recipe first.** Before you even get started, read the entire recipe. This is the number one way you'll be successful. It's like grade school when you took a test that began with "Read every question first." Remember that one? If you obeyed, you'd see that the only question you were to answer was "what's your name." Same thing goes with these recipes. By reading them first, you won't be surprised by ingredients, cooking tools, or cooking methods. You'll be prepared, and that's priceless when it comes to cooking.

2. **Don't be a victim to the recipe.** I love to play with food. That means I love experimentation and trial and error. I want you to do the same. Don't "not try" a recipe because it contains an ingredient you don't like. Instead, put your thinking cap on and ask, "Could I replace this ingredient with something else," or, "Could I eliminate this ingredient and get similar results?" What's the worst thing that happens: you try it and it doesn't work? Well, at least you'll know! And don't forget, I try not to leave you hanging. That's why I've offered several tips in the recipes.

3. **Take suggestions.** Most of these recipes offer a suggestion for the type of tortilla/taco shell to use. Again, this is my recommendation, but feel free to substitute with any of your favorites. Just because I like it doesn't mean you will. So go ahead, try that sprouted whole grain tortilla! Also, I provide recipes for making your own corn and flour tortillas (see pages 215 and 219)! I recommend you do that whenever you can. These tortillas taste *way* better than the store-bought versions. As for store-bought versions, I always recommend using a whole wheat or whole grain tortilla where a "tortilla" is called for in a recipe. There are more nutrients in a whole grain version than the white flour versions. I also recommend sticking with the 6-inch tacos size tortilla. Anything bigger and you've got a burrito!

4. *Mis en place.* Before you start cooking, prep all of your ingredients. This is called "mis en place," or "everything in its place." This practice helps you successfully execute any and every recipe you'll ever attempt, I promise.

5. **Leave it alone.** When it comes to cooking some foods, it's important to just leave it alone. Grilling, for example. If you fuss too much with the meat, fish, or poultry, you run the risk of it sticking to your grill. So set your timer and leave it be, ok?

6. **Get your pan hot!** A common mistake people make is not waiting long enough for the oil in their pan to get hot before they add the food. A cold pan will not cook your food properly, so wait until it's hot. It doesn't usually take more than a minute or two for that to happen, and you'll often be able to tell it's hot because the oil moves quickly in the pan and you'll notice it will start to shimmer and look almost wavy. That means it's ready!

7. **Let's talk salt.** I like salt, and I use it a lot in my recipes. You'll see here, though, that sometimes I say "season to taste." Or perhaps I don't call for an exact amount. That's by design. I know that some of you are pretty sensitive to salt, so I don't want to overwhelm you. I'm leaving *you* in charge of deciding how much salt something needs. But I always recommend tasting before adding any additional salt, because once salt is on your food, it's incredibly hard to get it off! And I like to use kosher salt. The bigger crystals make it easier to prevent over-salting, in my opinion.

8. **Use citrus!** You'll notice I use plenty of citrus juice in my recipes! That's for a good reason. The little hit of bright acidity that comes from them is such a compliment to almost any dish. So, wherever you see it, assume I mean *fresh* lime or lemon juice and not the jarred stuff—that stuff isn't as good. And while we're talking citrus, save or use the zest, too! Before juicing, remove the zest (just the yellow or green part, not the inner white part, which is bitter) and place it on a damp paper towel. Wrap it all in plastic wrap and store in a freezer bag in the freezer to use another time. And speaking of citrus, it might be helpful to know that one lime yields about two tablespoons fresh juice and one lemon yields about three tablespoons fresh juice.

9. **Following a specific diet?** While I don't call out allergens in this book, please know that many are naturally gluten-free and even dairy- and nut-free! And if they're not, you can easily adjust them to become allergen-free. For example, if you see "flour tortilla" called for in the ingredient list, swap in corn tortillas or use another gluten-free tortilla in its place.

10. **Most of the recipes in this book are designed to be the ENTIRE meal!** Great news, right? But I know some of you crave a little more, so along the way, I'll offer some suggestions as to what I would serve alongside the tacos. Here's a hint—you can never go wrong with an additional serving of vegetables!

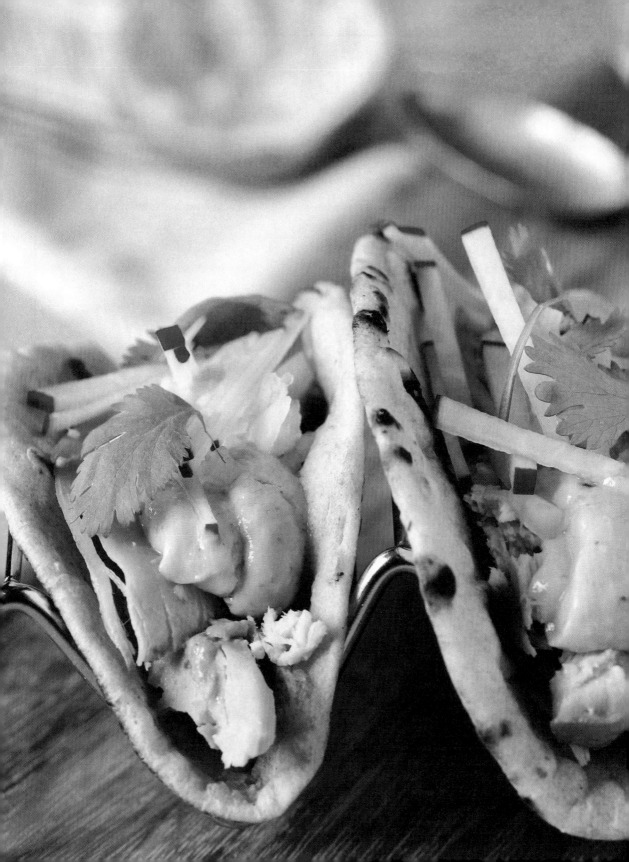

CHICKEN RECIPES

Chicken is a staple in my household. It's easy to cook and is the perfect platform for so many flavorful meals. This collection of chicken taco recipes is a blend of traditional and not-so-traditional chicken dishes. Don't miss my super easy recipes for Slow Cooker Chicken and Easy Poached Chicken—they'll make other recipes in this section come together quickly.

Super Simple Slow Cooker Chicken

MAKES: ABOUT 5½ CUPS SHREDDED CHICKEN

Your slow cooker is your best friend! Start this chicken in the morning so that when you get home from work, school, or your workout, you'll be steps away from dinner! This recipe was designed to be used in other recipes in the book, but feel free to customize and make it your own!

1 yellow or white onion, peeled, ends trimmed, and quartered

1½ pounds boneless, skinless chicken breasts

1½ pounds boneless, skinless chicken thighs

1 teaspoon kosher salt

2 cups low-sodium chicken broth

4 garlic cloves, peeled

1 jalapeño, stem removed, sliced in half (remove the membrane and seeds to reduce heat)

Scatter the onion pieces to cover the bottom of a 6-quart slow cooker. Top with the chicken and sprinkle with the salt. Pour the chicken broth around the chicken, then add the garlic and jalapeño, if using, and cover with the lid. Cook on low heat for 6 to 8 hours or on high heat for 3 to 4 hours.

Remove from slow cooker and pull apart using two forks. Season to taste with salt and pepper.

RECIPE NOTE: You'll find this recipe throughout the book being used in other recipes! That's why the flavor is mild. If you want to serve this chicken as-is, I would recommend one of the serving tips below, or be creative by making your own delicious combination.

SERVING TIP: The sky is the limit, but here are a few of my favorite combinations. Toss the chicken with salsa of your choice and serve in warmed tortillas topped with shredded lettuce, sour cream, and shredded cheese. Or toss chicken with fresh lime juice and cilantro then serve in warmed tortillas topped with freshly chopped tomatoes and spicy guacamole.

SAVING TIP: Store extra chicken in a sealable container for up to four days in the refrigerator and up to six months in the freezer.

Fire Roasted Tomato Salsa Chicken Tacos

SERVINGS: 4 TO 6

I love a good roasted tomato salsa. There's just something magical about that caramelization that happens in the oven! This one's easy to make, and I've paired it with the Slow Cooker Chicken to make a simple weeknight dinner.

For the salsa:

½ jalapeño, quartered (remove seeds and membrane for less heat)

2 cloves garlic, peeled

½ small white onion, chopped

2 teaspoons extra-virgin olive oil

1 (14.5-ounce) can fire roasted diced tomatoes

Juice of 1 lime

¼ cup packed cilantro, stems and leaves

¼ teaspoon kosher salt

For the tacos:

2 cups cooked shredded or chopped chicken, see Slow Cooker Chicken (see page 37) or Easy Poached Chicken (see page 49)

8 to 12 corn or flour tortillas, warmed

Toppings of your choice: shredded lettuce, sliced onion, shredded cheese, etc.

To make the salsa:

Toss jalapeño, garlic, and onion in oil. Move oven rack to the highest position, about 3 to 4 inches below heat source. Spread jalapeño mixture on a foil-lined sheet pan and broil 5 to 6 minutes, shaking the pan halfway through cooking time. Transfer to a blender, along with tomatoes and lime juice. Process until smooth. Add cilantro and salt, then pulse to combine.

To make the tacos:

Serve chicken in warmed tortillas with salsa and other toppings of your choice.

RECIPE NOTE: If you can't find fire roasted tomatoes at the store, don't sweat it. You can substitute a 14.5-ounce can of regular diced tomatoes for them.

COOKING TIP: For even more heat, don't remove the seeds or membrane from the jalapeño.

SAVING TIP: This makes about two cups of fresh salsa, but don't worry if you don't use it all! You can save it! Cover it and keep it in the fridge for up to five days.

Creamy Avocado Sauce Chicken Tacos

SERVINGS: 4 TO 6

Avocados are a staple in my household. I love their natural creaminess and their beautiful green color. Make sure you use ripe avocados for this recipe.

For the creamy avocado sauce:

1 large, ripe avocado

¼ cup plain Greek yogurt

1 (4-ounce) can diced green chiles

1 garlic clove, peeled

⅓ cup chopped white onion

¼ cup cilantro

1 lime, juice and zest

¼ teaspoon kosher salt

1 tablespoon water

For the tacos:

8 to 12 corn tortillas, warmed

2 cups cooked shredded or chopped chicken, warmed, see Slow Cooker Chicken (see page 37) or Easy Poached Chicken (see page 49)

Topping suggestions: cilantro, shredded romaine lettuce, thinly sliced radish, thinly sliced white onion, lime wedges, salsa, etc.

To make the creamy avocado sauce:

Scoop avocado flesh into a blender or the bowl of a food processor. Add the yogurt, green chiles, garlic, onion, cilantro, lime juice, lime zest, salt, and water. Puree until smooth, adding additional water by the tablespoon to thin, if desired.

To make the tacos:

Serve chicken in warmed tortillas with creamy avocado sauce, fresh cilantro leaves, thinly sliced romaine lettuce, radish, onion, or other toppings of your choice.

GROCERY TIP: How do you find the best avocado? Pick it up and feel it! If it gives slightly to the touch, it's ready. If it has any bruising or feels especially soft, it's over-ripe and not good anymore. If it's rock solid, you can still buy it—it just isn't ripe, so it won't be ready for a few days. To speed up the ripening process, place the firm avocado in a brown paper bag, along with an apple, fold over, and wait a day or so. Once ripened, use it or put it in the fridge. (Refer to page 5 for more Grocery Tips on stocking your fridge!)

RECIPE NOTE: This makes about 1¼ cup sauce.

RECIPE NOTE: Looking for a little more heat? Choose green chiles labeled "medium" or "hot" instead of mild.

SAVING TIP: Store extra sauce in an air-tight container for up to three days in the refrigerator.

Poppy Seed Chicken Tacos with Spinach, Strawberries, and Candied Pecans

SERVINGS: 4

This taco tastes like a delightful, summer salad, but in a tortilla! I love the addition of candied pecans here—they add the perfect crunch!

For the pecans:

2 tablespoons packed brown sugar

¼ teaspoon kosher salt

1 tablespoon water

1 cup pecan halves

For the dressing:

1 tablespoon + 1 teaspoon granulated sugar

2 tablespoons apple cider vinegar

1 teaspoon dry mustard powder

¼ cup vegetable oil

1 teaspoon shallot, grated or finely minced

1 teaspoon poppy seeds

For the tacos:

2 cups cooked chicken, chopped or pulled

8 large strawberries, stemmed and sliced

4 cups baby spinach

8 corn or flour tortillas, warmed

½ cup crumbled feta cheese

To make the pecans:

Place the brown sugar, salt, and water in a medium non-stick skillet. Mix together and cook over medium-high heat until bubbly. Add the pecans and cook 3 to 4 minutes, stirring often. Carefully remove the pecans from the pan and transfer to a wire rack lined with parchment paper (or foil that's been coated in nonstick cooking spray) to cool.

While pecans are cooling, make the dressing:

To a medium mixing bowl, add the sugar, vinegar, and mustard. Whisk in the oil, then add the shallot and poppy seeds. Remove 2 tablespoons, transferring them to a bowl large enough to hold the spinach and strawberries. Add the chicken to the bowl with the remaining dressing and toss to coat. Toss the spinach and strawberries with a pinch of salt and pepper, if desired.

To make the tacos:

Serve chicken on warmed tortillas, top with spinach mixture, and garnish with pecans and feta cheese.

RECIPE NOTE: Need cooked chicken for this dish? Use the Slow Cooker Chicken (see page 37) or Poached Chicken (see page 49) recipe or buy a rotisserie chicken at your grocery store.

SERVING TIP: If you don't feel like making the candied pecans, don't! This taco will taste just as good with plain or toasted pecans.

Curry Cashew Chicken Salad Tacos

SERVINGS: 4

I love the vibrant color and flavor of curry powder and always look forward to trying different variations. Seek out online retailers who make their own blends, or, if you've got the time, make your own!

For the dressing:

1 teaspoon extra-virgin olive oil

2 teaspoons curry powder

½ cup plain Greek yogurt

1 tablespoon fresh lime juice

¼ teaspoon lime zest

½ cup cilantro, chopped

For the chicken salad:

2 cups cooked chicken, cooled and chopped (see Slow Cooker Chicken, see page 37) or Easy Poached Chicken (see page 49)

½ cup cilantro, chopped

¼ cup dried apricots, chopped

¼ cup raw cashews, chopped

¼ cup diced red onion

½ cup diced red bell pepper

Kosher salt and freshly ground black pepper

For the tacos:

8 flour tortillas, warmed

4 cups shredded romaine lettuce

To toast the curry powder:

Set a small non-stick skillet over medium heat and add the oil. Once the oil is hot, add the curry powder and stir, cooking until fragrant, about 1 minute. Remove pan from the heat and allow to cool slightly.

To make the dressing:

In a medium bowl, mix together the Greek yogurt, lime juice and zest, cilantro, and the cooled curry mixture. (Dressing can also be pureed in a blender or food processor.)

To make the chicken salad:

To the bowl with the dressing, add the cooked chicken, cilantro, apricots, cashews, red onion, and red bell pepper. Toss to combine. Season to taste with salt and black pepper.

To make the tacos:

Serve the chicken salad on the tortillas topped with shredded lettuce.

COOKING TIP: Adjust the level of spice based on your preference. If you'd like a little more heat, go ahead and add a little more curry, but no more than 1 to 2 additional teaspoons.

Chicken Shawarma Tacos

SERVINGS: 4

The marinade for these shawarma tacos is so good, you might want to use it as a salad dressing, too! While this isn't authentic shawarma, you'll get some of the same flavors that are signature to the dish.

1 ¼ pounds boneless, skinless chicken breasts

For the marinade:

¼ cup plain Greek yogurt

2 tablespoons fresh lemon juice

2 tablespoons extra-virgin olive oil

1 teaspoon ground turmeric

1 teaspoon ground cumin

½ teaspoon ground cinnamon

1 clove garlic, minced

For the yogurt sauce:

⅓ cup + 1 tablespoon plain Greek yogurt

2 tablespoons + 1 teaspoon tahini

2 cloves garlic

2 tablespoons fresh lemon juice

¼ cup fresh parsley, roughly chopped

⅛ teaspoon kosher salt

To prepare the chicken:

Slice the chicken breasts, lengthwise, into three to four 1½ to 2-inch strips.

To make the marinade:

In a medium mixing bowl, whisk together all of the marinade ingredients. Add chicken to the bowl and toss to coat. Cover and refrigerate for at least 1 hour and up to 8 hours.

While chicken is marinating, make the yogurt sauce:

In the bowl of a small food processor add the yogurt, tahini, garlic, lemon juice, parsley, and salt. Puree until smooth. Yogurt sauce can be made up to one day in advance. Store in the refrigerator and stir before using.

To cook the chicken:

Preheat the grill to medium-high heat or set a grill pan over medium-high heat. If using a grill, clean the grill grates and brush them with oil. If using a grill pan, coat pan lightly in oil. Remove chicken from marinade and pat dry; discard marinade. Thread chicken lengthwise onto skewers. Sprinkle with salt.

Grill the chicken, turning once, until internal temperature reaches 165°F, 8 to 10 minutes total.

. . . continued on next page

For the tacos:

4 whole wheat naan, sliced in half vertically, warmed

1 cup chopped tomatoes

2 cups chopped romaine lettuce

1 lemon, cut into wedges

Special equipment:

6 wooden skewers, soaked in water for 30 minutes

To make the tacos:

Remove chicken from skewers and place on warmed naan. Top with tomatoes and romaine lettuce then drizzle with yogurt sauce. Serve with lemon wedge.

PREP TIP: To make slicing chicken easier, partially freeze and then cut it. The sauce can also be made using a stick blender or by hand. If making by hand, be sure to chop parsley fine.

ALTERNATE COOKING INFORMATION: Don't feel like grilling? Bake these instead! Prepare the same, but without skewering chicken pieces. Place chicken on a foil-lined baking sheet coated with non-stick spray and bake in a 425°F oven for 20 to 25 minutes, flipping halfway through cooking time.

RECIPE NOTE: If you don't have a food processor, you can easily make the sauce in a bowl with a whisk. Just be sure to finely chop the parsley before adding it.

Easy Poached Chicken

SERVINGS: 4 TO 6

Poaching chicken is easy and fast! Get it started before working on the rest of your meal, and by the time you've got it all ready, your chicken will be ready, too. Feel free to use this recipe whenever "cooked chicken" is called for in other recipes in this book.

1¼ to 1½ pounds boneless, skinless chicken breast

½ white onion peeled, ends trimmed, and quartered

1 garlic clove, smashed

8 whole black peppercorns

3 sprigs of fresh thyme, optional

Kosher salt and freshly ground black pepper

Place chicken breasts in a deep-sided skillet. Add the onion, garlic, black peppercorns, and fresh thyme, scattering over the chicken breasts. Add water to the skillet, just enough to fully cover the chicken, and set over medium-high heat. Once boiling, reduce heat so liquid is just simmering (little bubbles will start to appear, but will not be as aggressive as a boil), partially cover, and cook about 10 minutes, ensuring liquid stays at a simmer. Check the temperature of the chicken; it should be 165°F. If not, continue cooking for a few additional minutes. Allow chicken to cool before shredding or chopping. Season to taste with salt and pepper.

RECIPE NOTE: You'll find this recipe throughout the book for use in other recipes! That's why the flavor is mild. If you want to serve this chicken as is, I would recommend one of the serving ideas below. Or be creative and make your own delicious combination.

SERVING TIP: Serve cooked chicken in tortillas or taco shells with traditional taco accoutrements—salsa, lettuce, tomatoes, shredded cheese, or any other of your favorite ingredients.

SAVING TIP: Store extra chicken in a sealable container for up to four days in the refrigerator and up to six months in the freezer.

Honey Mustard Pretzel Chicken Tender Tacos

SERVINGS: 4

For the chicken:

½ cup plain Greek yogurt

1 tablespoon + 2 teaspoons honey

1 tablespoon +1 teaspoon Dijon mustard

1 tablespoon apple cider vinegar

1 teaspoon water

2 cloves garlic, minced

¼ cup whole wheat flour

1½ cups (2 ounces) pretzels, crushed

1 pound chicken tenders

½ teaspoon kosher salt

For the salad topping:

4 cups chopped romaine lettuce

1 medium red, yellow or orange bell pepper, sliced

½ cucumber, thinly sliced

1 cup thinly sliced red onion

For the tacos:

8 corn or flour tortillas, warmed

1 cup (1⅓ ounces) pretzels, lightly crushed

Who doesn't love chicken tenders? That crunchy breading is divine! So why not turn one of your favorite meals into tacos? I pair them with a delightful honey mustard sauce that also acts as a delicious coating for the chicken.

To make the chicken:

Preheat the oven to 400°F and line a baking sheet with foil. Coat the foil liberally with non-stick cooking spray.

Whisk together the yogurt, honey, mustard, vinegar, water, and garlic in a small mixing bowl. Remove half and reserve.

Place the flour in a shallow dish and add the crushed pretzels to a separate shallow dish. Season the tenders with salt, then dredge, one at a time, in the flour mixture; dip into the yogurt mixture, and then coat with the crushed pretzels. Place tenders on the prepared pan and bake for 15 to 20 minutes, or until internal temperature reaches 165°F, turning once halfway through cooking time.

To make the salad topping:

Combine the lettuce, peppers, cucumber, and onions in a large bowl. Add the reserved dressing and toss to coat.

To make the tacos:

Serve the chicken tenders in warmed tortillas topped with the salad. Garnish with lightly crushed pretzels.

GROCERY TIP: Chicken tenders are often more expensive than buying chicken breasts. If you have a little extra time, buy chicken breasts and simply cut them into strips the size of tenders!

Bahn Mi Chicken Tacos

SERVINGS: 4

For the marinade:

2 cloves garlic, smashed

2 green onions (white and light green parts only), sliced (reserve half for garnish)

¼ cup vegetable oil

3 tablespoons low-sodium soy sauce

2 tablespoons packed light brown sugar

1 bird's eye chile or serrano pepper, thinly sliced

1 ¼ pounds boneless, skinless chicken breast, pounded to ½-inch thickness

For the Sriracha dressing:

¼ cup + 2 tablespoons plain Greek yogurt

2 teaspoons Sriracha

1 clove garlic, smashed and finely chopped

1 tablespoon fresh lemon juice

Pinch kosher salt

For the tacos:

½ cucumber, thinly sliced

1 cup fresh cilantro leaves

1 jalapeño, sliced, optional

4 radishes, thinly sliced

1 cup shredded carrots

8 corn tortillas or 4 whole wheat naan cut in half, warmed

A bahn mi is a culmination of delightful flavors. I love the balance of tartness, spiciness, and freshness. These tacos are a salute to one of my favorite sandwiches.

To make the marinade:

In a medium bowl, whisk together the garlic, onion, oil, soy sauce, sugar, and chile. Reserve ¼ cup of the marinade and place the remaining mixture in a gallon-size, sealable plastic bag. Add the chicken, press out any excess air from the bag, then seal and turn to coat. Marinate in the refrigerator for at least 30 minutes and up to 2 hours.

To cook the chicken:

Preheat the grill to medium-high heat or set a grill pan over medium-high heat. If using a grill, clean the grill grates and brush them with oil. If using a grill pan, coat pan lightly in oil. Remove chicken from marinade and pat dry; discard the marinade. Grill the chicken, turning once, until internal temperature reaches 165°F, 10 to 12 minutes total. Let rest 5 minutes before slicing into thin strips.

To make the Sriracha dressing:

To a small bowl, add the Greek yogurt, Sriracha, garlic, lemon juice, and salt. Mix to combine.

To make the tacos:

Toss the cucumber, cilantro, jalapeño, radishes, and carrots with the reserved dressing. Serve the chicken on the tortillas, topped with the dressed vegetables and garnished with the Sriracha dressing.

. . . continued on next page

GROCERY TIP: If you can't find any bird's eye chiles or serrano peppers at your store, use half a jalapeño pepper in its place. To replicate the heat from the bird's eye chiles or serrano, don't remove the seeds or membrane of the jalapeño before slicing.

ALTERNATE COOKING INFORMATION: No grill? No problem! You can bake this dish, too. Place chicken on a foil lined baking sheet coated with non-stick spray and bake at 425°F for 20 to 25 minutes, flipping halfway through cooking time.

COOKING TIP: Don't feel like whisking? You can puree the marinade in a blender or food processor, as well.

KITCHEN TIP: Did you know that one lemon yields about three tablespoons of fresh lemon juice? Now you do!

Grilled Chicken Caesar Salad Taco

SERVINGS: 4

Growing up I ate so many Caesar salads, and I just loved them. Something about that garlic and Parmesan cheese made me happy. You'll notice I use anchovies in this recipe, but don't let that scare you—I promise, they're delicious!

For the dressing/marinade:

1 clove garlic, smashed and minced

3 anchovy fillets, drained of oil

¾ cup plain Greek yogurt

2 teaspoons Dijon mustard

2 tablespoons fresh lemon juice

¼ teaspoon kosher salt

½ teaspoon freshly ground black pepper

For the chicken:

1¼ pounds boneless, skinless chicken breast, pounded to ¼-inch thickness

For the tacos:

6 ounces romaine lettuce, cleaned and chopped (about 6 cups chopped)

1 cup cherry tomatoes, halved (or about 1 cup chopped tomatoes)

½ cup shredded Parmesan cheese

8 hard taco shells, warmed

Freshly ground black pepper

To make the dressing:

Chop the garlic with the anchovies, then, using the side of a knife, smash into a paste. To a small mixing bowl, add the garlic-anchovy mixture, yogurt, mustard, lemon juice, salt, and pepper. Whisk until combined. Remove and reserve ¼ cup of the dressing and place the remaining marinade in a gallon-size, sealable plastic bag.

To marinate the chicken:

Add the pounded chicken to the bag with the dressing. Press out any excess air from the bag, then seal and turn to coat. Marinate for 2 to 4 hours in the refrigerator.

To cook the chicken:

Preheat the grill to medium-high heat or set a grill pan over medium-high heat. If using a grill, clean the grill grates and brush them with oil. If using a grill pan, coat pan lightly in oil. Remove the chicken from marinade and pat dry; discard marinade. Grill the chicken, turning once, until internal temperature reaches 165°F, 10 to 12 minutes total. Transfer chicken to a cutting board and let rest 5 minutes before slicing.

To make the tacos:

To a large bowl, add the lettuce, tomatoes, and Parmesan cheese. Add the sliced chicken and remaining dressing and toss to coat.

Serve Caesar salad in warmed taco shells topped with a little freshly ground black pepper and enjoy!

PREP TIP: Pounding chicken is simple and makes it so the chicken cooks evenly and quickly. I like to do this by placing the chicken breasts in a gallon-size, sealable plastic bag, one or two at a time, then pound to desired thickness using a rolling pin or a meat mallet.

PREP TIP: What to do while you're waiting for your chicken to marinate? Great question! I like to use that time to get my lettuce chopped and my tomatoes cut. Work smarter, not harder!

ALTERNATE COOKING INFORMATION: Want to bring it inside? Set your grill pan or skillet over medium-high heat. Add 1 to 2 teaspoons vegetable oil and cook the chicken 5 to 6 minutes each side, or until internal temperature reaches 165°F.

RECIPE NOTE: If anchovies aren't your thing, you can leave them out. But here's the deal, they're DELICIOUS, and you should really use them in this recipe!

COOKING TIP: Feeling really bold? Go ahead and grill the romaine lettuce, too! Just brush the whole head with olive oil, then place the whole head on the grill and give it a few minutes to cook!

Slow Cooker Poblano Chicken Tacos

SERVINGS: 8

Looking for a new way to make slow cooker chicken? Why not try adding a few poblanos into the mix? Roasting them with some onions and garlic before pureeing them into a sauce is a great way to easily build flavor. Those flavors build even more when they simmer with chicken in your slow cooker all day. Truly an easy and delicious meal!

For the sauce:

1 small white onion, quartered

2 poblano peppers, seeded and diced

2 cloves garlic, peeled

1 tablespoon extra-virgin olive oil

Kosher salt and freshly ground black pepper

1 (4-ounce) can diced green chiles

For the chicken:

2 pounds boneless, skinless chicken breast

¼ teaspoon kosher salt

⅛ teaspoon freshly ground black pepper

For the tacos:

16 flour tortillas, warmed

Optional toppings: chopped cilantro, diced avocado, shredded cabbage, jalapeño slices

To make the sauce:

Position oven rack 5 to 6 inches from the heating element and preheat the broiler.

To a large bowl, add the onion, poblano, and garlic. Add the oil and toss to combine. Season lightly with salt and pepper. Broil for 10 minutes, stirring halfway through cooking time. Remove from oven and allow to cool slightly.

Add the cooled, broiled onion and poblano to a blender along with ¼ cup water and puree until smooth. Use caution, as hot foods release steam, which increases pressure. Be sure food is cooled and that blender lid has a vent for steam to escape.

To cook the chicken:

Place the chicken in a 6-quart slow cooker, season with salt and freshly ground black pepper. Pour poblano sauce over chicken. Cover with a lid and cook on low for 8 hours.

To make the tacos:

Using two forks, pull chicken apart to shred. This can be done in the slow cooker. Serve chicken in warm tortillas with cilantro, diced avocado, shredded cabbage, and jalapeño slices.

. . . continued on next page

GROCERY TIP: I love using a mixture of chicken breasts and thighs for this dish—you'll get a great chicken flavor this way.

SERVING TIP: This tastes even more fabulous when you finish the chicken with a big hit of fresh lime juice just before serving!

INGREDIENT TIP: True or false? All peppers are spicy. FALSE! Poblanos are actually not spicy at all. They have a Scoville rating (a scale that rates peppers based on their level of capsaicin, or "hot stuff" compound) of about 1,000–2,000 SHU (Scoville Heat Units). For comparison, a jalapeño can be as much as 50,000 SHU[*]. So fear not, spice-adverse taco lovers, you can safely enjoy this recipe!

---

[*] www.chilefacts.nmsu.edu

Jerk Chicken Tacos with Mango Avocado Salsa

SERVINGS: 4

Spicy meets sweet in this delicious taco riff. Don't cringe at that marinade ingredient list—I know it's long, but you likely have some of the ingredients already on hand. I recommend doubling this recipe, because you'll want this again tomorrow night!

For the marinade:

1 teaspoon ground cinnamon

1 tablespoon packed light brown sugar

¼ teaspoon ground allspice

½ teaspoon dried thyme leaves

2 cloves garlic, peeled and smashed

2 scallions, white and green parts only, thinly sliced

1 2-inch knob of fresh ginger, peeled and roughly chopped

2 Scotch bonnet or habanero peppers, stems removed and roughly chopped

¼ cup canola oil

1 tablespoon fresh lime juice

1 ¼ pounds boneless, skinless chicken breast

To make the marinade:

To a blender or bowl of a small food processor, add the cinnamon, brown sugar, allspice, thyme, garlic, scallions, ginger, peppers, oil and lime juice. Puree until smooth. Transfer the marinade to a gallon-size, sealable bag. Add the chicken, press out any excess air from the bag, then seal and turn to coat. Marinate for at least 1 hour and up to 24 hours in the refrigerator.

To make the mango avocado salsa:

Combine the mango, avocado, onion, cilantro, lime zest, and lime juice in a bowl. Toss to combine. Season with salt, as needed.

To cook the chicken:

Preheat the grill to medium-high heat or set a grill pan over medium-high heat. If using a grill, clean the grill grates and brush them with oil. If using a grill pan, coat pan lightly with oil. Once hot, remove the chicken from the marinade and pat dry; discard marinade. Season with a little kosher salt. Grill the chicken, turning once, until internal temperature reaches 165°F, 10 to 14 minutes total. Remove from grill and let rest 5 minutes before slicing.

. . . continued on next page

For the mango avocado salsa:

1 ripe mango, peeled and diced

1 ripe avocado, seeded and diced

¼ cup finely chopped red onion

¼ cup packed, fresh cilantro leaves, roughly chopped

1 teaspoon lime zest

1 tablespoon fresh lime juice

For the tacos:

8 corn tortillas, warmed

To make the tacos:

Serve sliced chicken in warmed tortillas and top with mango avocado salsa.

GROCERY TIP: If you can't find fresh mango, substitute with thawed, frozen mango. Or swap in a different fruit for the mango. Pineapple would also work well here, as well as melon.

RECIPE NOTE: Scotch bonnet and habanero peppers are SUPER spicy. If you're not into that much heat, you can replace either one with jalapeño peppers.

Dad's Sesame Soy Chicken Tacos

SERVINGS: 6

For the chicken:

1½ pounds boneless, skinless chicken thighs or breasts

½ cup low-sodium soy sauce

2 tablespoons packed light brown sugar

2 tablespoons extra-virgin olive oil

4 garlic cloves, minced

2 teaspoons Sriracha

2 tablespoons Hoisin sauce

2 tablespoons fresh ginger, peeled and grated

For the slaw:

2 teaspoons fresh ginger, grated

1 tablespoon rice vinegar

1 teaspoon sesame oil

1 tablespoon white sesame seeds, toasted, if desired

2 cups coleslaw mix, or about 2 cups of your favorite veggies, shredded

For the sauce:

¼ cup reserved marinade

1 teaspoon Dijon mustard

For the tacos:

12 flour tortillas, warmed

My dad is kind of a foodie, too, and he actually created this recipe! I learned to love food because of him (and my mom) and I love this recipe he created that combines some of my favorite flavors.

To prepare the chicken:

Place chicken in a gallon-size, sealable bag and pound to ¼-inch thickness. In a medium bowl, whisk together the soy sauce, brown sugar, olive oil, garlic, Sriracha, Hoisin, and ginger. Reserve ¼ cup of the marinade and set aside. Transfer the remaining marinade to the bag with the chicken, press out any excess air from the bag, then seal and turn to coat. Marinate for at least 1 hour and up to 6 hours in the refrigerator.

To cook the chicken:

Preheat the grill to medium-high heat or set a grill pan over medium-high heat. If using grill, clean the grill grates and brush them with oil. If using a grill pan, coat pan lightly with oil. Remove chicken from the marinade and pat dry; discard the marinade. Grill the chicken, turning once, until internal temperature reaches 165°F, 10 to 14 minutes total. Transfer chicken to a cutting board and let rest 5 minutes before slicing.

To make the slaw:

To a large mixing bowl, add the ginger, vinegar, oil, and sesame seeds and whisk together. Add the coleslaw mix and toss to combine.

To make the tacos:

Whisk the mustard into the reserved marinade. Serve the chicken on the warmed tortillas, then top with slaw and a drizzle of reserved marinade.

PREP TIP: Having a hard time peeling that ginger? Try using a spoon! It sometimes works better than that paring knife for this task.

ALTERNATE COOKING INFORMATION: Remove chicken from marinade and place on a foil-lined baking sheet. Bake at 400°F for 15 minutes, or until internal temp reaches 165°F, flipping halfway through cooking time. Let rest 5 minutes before slicing.

RECIPE NOTE: I like to use shredded cabbage and carrots for the slaw. But take the advice of my sister-in-law and add in snow pea shoots or even kohlrabi!

Sausage, Kale and Sweet Onion Tacos

SERVINGS: 4

Tired of kale? Me neither! I love its earthy flavor and fun texture, and it works really well when paired with the brilliant flavors of sausage and onion. If you don't like kale, trust me, you'll like it this way!

For the sausage:

1 tablespoon + 2 teaspoons extra-virgin olive oil, divided

1 sweet Vidalia onion, sliced, about 2 cups

¼ teaspoon kosher salt

2 links pre-cooked chicken sausage, sliced ¼-inch thick

1 clove garlic, minced

1 small bunch of Tuscan or dinosaur kale, stems removed and thinly sliced, about 4 cups

1 teaspoon dried thyme leaves

2 teaspoons red wine vinegar

For the tacos:

2 ounces goat cheese, crumbled

8 corn or flour tortillas, warmed

To cook the taco mixture:

Set a large skillet over medium-high heat. Add 1 tablespoon oil along with the onions and cook for 5 minutes, or until slightly softened. Add salt, turn heat down to low then cover with a lid or foil and cook an additional 20 minutes, stirring occasionally.

Transfer onions to a bowl and turn the heat back up to medium-high. Add remaining 2 teaspoons olive oil. Once hot, add the sausage and cook for 3 minutes, until lightly browned. Reduce heat to medium, add the kale and garlic, and cook 2 to 3 minutes. Add the thyme and the onions and reduce the heat to low, cover, and cook an additional minute. Remove from heat and stir in red wine vinegar. Season to taste with salt and black pepper.

To make the tacos:

Serve the sausage mixture in warmed tortillas and garnish with crumbled goat cheese.

GROCERY TIP: Choose the sausage flavor of your choice here. I personally love a spicy sausage or a sweet Italian version.

SERVING TIP: Buy an extra bunch of kale and make kale chips to serve alongside these tacos. Add the stemmed, chopped kale to a large bowl and toss with 2 teaspoons olive oil and a pinch of salt. Spread the kale out onto a large baking sheet lined with parchment paper and bake at 375°F for 10 minutes, or until crispy.

TURKEY AND LAMB RECIPES

Turkey isn't just for Thanksgiving! It's the perfect filling for tacos! And I've used it in some pretty untraditional ways in this book. From riffs on sandwiches to spicy homemade chili, there's something in here for everyone!

Italian Meatball Tacos

SERVINGS: 6

Doubters don't doubt! Meatballs are actually a PERFECT taco filling. These little guys are made with lean ground turkey and sausage and are paired with your favorite marinara. It's a little taste of Italia wrapped in a tortilla!

For the meatballs:

¾ cup plain breadcrumbs

¼ cup milk

1 pound lean ground turkey

½ pound lean ground pork or turkey sausage

1 large egg, lightly beaten

1 teaspoon Italian seasoning

1 clove garlic, finely chopped

⅓ cup finely chopped white onion

¾ teaspoon kosher salt

¼ teaspoon freshly ground black pepper

2 tablespoons grated Parmesan cheese, plus extra for garnish

5 ounces frozen spinach, thawed and drained of any excess moisture

For the tacos:

12 corn tortillas, warmed

2 cups marinara of your choice, warmed

½ cup chopped parsley, for garnish

To make the meatballs:

Preheat the oven to 400°F. Line a large baking sheet with foil and spray with non-stick cooking spray.

Add the breadcrumbs to a large bowl, along with the milk, and stir to combine. Let soak for about 8 to 10 minutes, until breadcrumbs are moistened.

To the bowl with the breadcrumbs, add the ground turkey and sausage, along with the egg, Italian seasoning, garlic, onion, salt, pepper, Parmesan cheese, and spinach. Using lightly oiled hands, shape mixture into 1½ -inch balls and place on prepared baking sheet. Bake for 15 to 18 minutes, or until internal temperature reaches 165°F.

To make the tacos:

Serve meatballs in warmed tortillas and top with marinara sauce, Parmesan cheese, and chopped parsley.

GROCERY TIP: Worried about choosing the "right" marinara? Take a look at the label. My vote is always for the one that has the fewest ingredients along with very little sodium. I like salt, but I want to be the one adding it!

GROCERY TIP: Frozen spinach usually comes in a 10-ounce bag or box. I recommend buying the bag, removing half for this recipe, and then saving the other half in the freezer for the next time you make these tacos.

. . . continued on next page

GROCERY TIP: Use whole wheat bread crumbs for a nutritious twist. Gluten free? No problem! Swap in gluten free bread crumbs or pulse some gluten free bread in a food processor to make your own bread crumbs!

COOKING TIP: Make sure your spinach is fully drained. You can release the liquid by using a mesh strainer. After that, wrap it in a few clean paper towels and squeeze out the remaining moisture.

COOKING TIP: Keep your meatballs warm by dropping them in the warmed sauce about 5 minutes before serving time.

SERVING TIP: Pair these tacos with a big, hearty salad, loaded with your favorite vegetables.

BWLT Tacos

SERVINGS: 4

Was that a mistake? Did I accidentally insert a "W" into my "BLT?" Nope, that "W" is intentional and it stands for "watermelon." Trust me, it's the perfect balance to that salty bacon, and you'll love the lime chili mayo that accompanies it!

For the lime chili mayo:

3 tablespoons mayonnaise

2 tablespoons plain Greek yogurt

¼ cup cilantro, chopped, plus extra for garnish

¼ teaspoon chili powder

2 tablespoons fresh lime juice

For the tacos:

8 slices turkey bacon

1 head Romaine lettuce, cleaned and chopped into bite size pieces

2 large ripe tomatoes, sliced ¼-inch thick, then cut in half

8 seedless watermelon slices, ½-inch, rind removed and sliced into strips

8 corn tortillas, warmed

To make the lime chili mayo:

To a small bowl, add the mayonnaise, yogurt, cilantro, chili powder, and lime juice. Whisk to combine and season to taste with salt and black pepper.

To cook the bacon:

Set a large non-stick skillet over medium heat. Add half of the bacon and cook turning frequently until crisp, about 8 to 10 minutes. Using tongs, transfer bacon to a paper towel lined plate. Cover the bacon with another paper towel and pat dry. Repeat the process with the remaining bacon.

To make the tacos:

Place cooked bacon down the middle of each tortilla, then top with lettuce, tomatoes, and watermelon. Drizzle the lime chili mayo over the top and garnish with cilantro.

SERVING TIP: Want to go tortilla-less? Try this one using the romaine or even tomato as your veggie-based tortilla. Simply leave romaine leaves intact and build tacos on leaves. For the tomatoes, slice ½-inch thick, then fill and enjoy!

Sliced Turkey Taco with Special Sauce

SERVINGS: 4

For the sauce:

2 tablespoons ketchup

¼ cup + 1 tablespoon mayonnaise

1 teaspoon granulated sugar or honey

¼ teaspoon paprika

⅛ teaspoon ground cayenne pepper, if desired

¼ teaspoon garlic powder

¼ teaspoon onion powder

¼ teaspoon dried thyme leaves

½ teaspoon dried ground oregano

For the tacos:

2 whole wheat naan

12 ounces roasted turkey, thinly sliced

4 (1-ounce) slices provolone cheese or ½ cup shredded mild cheddar cheese

4 cups thinly sliced romaine lettuce

1 tomato, thinly sliced

½ red onion, thinly sliced

¼ cup dill pickle slices

¼ cup sprouts

When I was in college, there was a delicious little sandwich place that I used to frequent. I loved it and spent most of any of the money I earned on their sandwiches. I wanted to re-create that sandwich in this recipe, but this time in taco form. The result? Let's just say I'm glad I don't have to pinch pennies to buy them anymore!

To make the sauce:

In a small bowl, whisk together the ketchup, mayonnaise, sugar, and remaining spices. Set aside or cover and refrigerate if not eating immediately.

To make the tacos:

Toast the naan, then slice in half vertically. Top each naan half with turkey, cheese, lettuce, tomato, onion, pickles, and sprouts. Drizzle with sauce.

COOKING TIP: The sauce gets better with time. Make it ahead to allow flavors to deepen.

COOKING TIP: Want to make your own pickles? It's easy! To a very clean 1-pint jar, add enough thinly sliced cucumbers to fill just 1 inch below top. Add 5 to 6 black peppercorns, ½ teaspoon mustard seeds, and a few sprigs of really clean fresh dill. To a saucepan, add ¾ cup white vinegar, ⅔ cup water, and 1 teaspoon kosher salt. Bring to a boil, then pour over cucumbers. Liquid should cover cucumbers completely. Cool on the counter for 1 hour. Once cool to the touch, tightly screw on the lid and move to the refrigerator and store for about two days before opening.

SERVING TIP: Use as many or few toppings on this taco as you like—they're just a suggestion!

SERVING TIP: Need a side? Serve up a big bowl of fruit salad alongside these tacos!

Avocado Basil Turkey Tacos

SERVINGS: 4

Basil happens to be one of my favorite herbs, and I love it with juicy, ripe tomatoes and creamy, fresh mozzarella cheese. For a satisfying twist, I added turkey and a little avocado, and of course, piled it all on a tortilla!

For the dressing:

½ ripe avocado

1 tablespoon extra-virgin olive oil

1 cup fresh basil, lightly packed

3 tablespoons extra-virgin olive oil mayonnaise or other mayonnaise

3 tablespoons water

⅛ teaspoon kosher salt

Freshly ground black pepper

For the salad:

4 cups baby spinach, thinly sliced

½ small red onion, thinly sliced

1 ripe tomato, chopped

4 ounces fresh mozzarella, chopped

1 cup fresh basil, thinly sliced

1 tablespoon red wine vinegar

For the tacos:

12 ounces roasted turkey breast, thinly sliced

8 flour tortillas, warmed or room temperature

To make the dressing:

Scoop the avocado flesh into a food processor or blender along with the oil, basil, mayonnaise, and water. Blend until smooth. Season with salt and pepper.

To make the salad:

To a large mixing bowl, add the spinach, onion, tomato, mozzarella, and basil, then toss with the red wine vinegar.

To make the tacos:

Spread the avocado mixture evenly down the center of each tortilla, then top with the turkey and the spinach mixture.

GROCERY TIP: For the turkey, you can use the deli varieties or purchase a cooked turkey breast that you can slice at home.

COOKING TIP: To thinly slice basil (also called chiffonade), gather basil leaves and stack them on top of each other. Roll up lengthwise, then slice across the rolled leaves. You'll be rewarded with "ribbons" of basil.

Mom's Chili Tacos

SERVINGS: 6

My mom's chili is GOOD. Remember when I told you it was one of my favorite meals? It still is! While this isn't her recipe, it was created in honor of her famous pot of goodness. And I love how perfect chili tastes in warmed tortillas! It's comforting and delicious.

For the chili:

1 tablespoon extra-virgin olive oil

1 pound lean ground turkey

1 small white onion, finely chopped (save ¼ cup for serving)

2 tablespoons chili powder (medium or hot)

1 tablespoon ground cumin

1 teaspoon ground cinnamon

2 teaspoons cocoa powder

1 (14.5-ounce) can diced tomatoes

1 (15-ounce) can kidney beans, drained and rinsed

1 tablespoon packed light brown sugar

Kosher salt

For the tacos:

12 corn or flour tortillas

Optional toppings: shredded cheese, tomatoes, avocados, plain Greek yogurt

To make the chili:

Set a large saucepan or pot over medium-high heat and add the oil. Once hot, add the ground turkey and cook, breaking up the meat with a spoon, until browned and no longer pink, about 10 minutes. Add the onion and cook about 5 to 6 minutes, until onions are softened. Add the chili powder, cumin, cinnamon, and cocoa powder and cook about 2 minutes, stirring occasionally. Stir in the diced tomatoes, beans, and brown sugar. Reduce heat to medium-low and cook, partially covered, about 20 to 30 minutes and up to 1 hour.

Remove lid and turn up the heat towards the end of cooking to "cook off" some of the extra liquid. (You'll want this to be thick so that it stays in your tortilla!) Season to taste with salt.

To make the tacos:

Serve the chili in warmed tortillas and top with your favorite fixings!

GROCERY TIP: Not in the mood for turkey? These can easily be made using ground beef, ground chicken, or ground pork. Want to go meatless? Swap in some tofu crumbles!

GROCERY TIP: For this recipe, I recommend you use 85% or 93% lean ground turkey. Extra lean, or 99% lean, won't have enough fat and will stick to your pan.

Italian Turkey Sausage Pizza Taco

SERVINGS: 4

Is it a pizza or is it a taco? Perhaps this recipe is a stretch when it comes to being called a taco, but I think it works! It just goes to show that you can turn almost anything into a taco! And I love using ground sausage here; it certainly helps elicit that "pizza" feeling.

For the pizza topping:

1 tablespoon extra-virgin olive oil

1 small shallot, diced

4 ounces mushrooms, chopped

⅛ teaspoon kosher salt

½ pound ground hot or sweet turkey Italian sausage

2 cups baby spinach, thinly sliced

For making the tacos:

½ cup marinara sauce

¼ cup shredded Asiago cheese

½ cup shredded mozzarella cheese

½ cup fresh basil, thinly sliced

Yogurt flatbreads (see page 230) or pitas, cut into 6-inch circles or squares (or really whatever works, as long as you've got 4 total)

Preheat the oven to 425°F. Set a large sheet pan in the oven while it preheats.

To make the pizza topping:

Set a large, non-stick skillet over medium heat and add the oil. Once hot, add the shallot and cook 2 minutes, until softened. Add the mushrooms and salt and cook an additional 2 to 3 minutes. Add sausage and cook, stirring to crumble, until browned, about 3 to 4 minutes. Adjust heat if scorching begins to happen. Once sausage is cooked through and no longer pink, carefully drain excess fat. Remove from heat and stir in the spinach.

To make the tacos:

Remove pan from the oven and carefully place flatbreads or pita on it. Spread 2 tablespoons marinara sauce on each flatbread then top with sausage mixture. Sprinkle with cheese and place in the oven. Bake for about 10 to 12 minutes, or until cheese is melted and golden.

Remove the pan from the oven. Garnish pizzas with basil then fold up and serve.

GROCERY TIP: Can't find ground sausage? No problem. Buy raw links instead and just remove from the casing before cooking.

Lamb Tacos with Cucumber Yogurt Salad

SERVINGS: 4

There's something so fabulous about creamy yogurt paired with fresh parsley and mint. Toss it with cucumber, onions, and tomatoes and it becomes the perfect complement to the spice-infused lamb in this recipe.

For the salad:

1 clove garlic, minced

¼ cup + ½ cup plain Greek yogurt

⅓ cup lightly packed fresh mint, chopped

½ cup lightly packed fresh parsley, finely chopped

2 tablespoons fresh lemon juice

¼ teaspoon kosher salt

Freshly ground black pepper

2 large tomatoes, seeded and chopped

½ small white onion, thinly sliced

1 small cucumber, halved and thinly sliced

For the lamb:

1 ¼ pounds ground lamb

1 clove garlic, minced

½ teaspoon ground coriander

½ teaspoon ground cardamom

⅛ teaspoon crushed red pepper

¼ cup plain Greek yogurt

To make the salad:

In a large mixing bowl, whisk together the garlic along with the yogurt, mint, parsley, and lemon juice. Season with salt and black pepper. Add the tomatoes, onion, and cucumber and toss to combine. Cover and refrigerate.

To cook the lamb:

Set a large skillet over medium-high heat. Add the ground lamb and cook, breaking up the meat with a spoon, until browned, about 10 to 12 minutes. Drain most of the fat from the pan, then add the garlic along with the coriander, cardamom, and crushed red pepper. Cook, stirring occasionally, until fragrant, about 2 minutes. Turn heat to low, add the plain Greek yogurt, water, and fresh lemon juice, cover and keep warm until ready to serve.

To make the tacos:

Serve lamb mixture into warmed tortillas topped with cucumber mixture.

PREP TIP: Want to add some plant protein? Make these Crispy Chickpeas: Drain and rinse one 15-ounce can of chickpeas. Toss with 1 tablespoon olive oil and ¼ teaspoon kosher salt, ¼ teaspoon black pepper, and ½ teaspoon Italian seasoning or dried oregano. Spread out onto a baking sheet and bake at 400°F for 20 minutes, stirring halfway through cooking time.

3 tablespoons water

1 tablespoon fresh lemon juice

¼ teaspoon kosher salt

For the tacos:

8 flour tortillas

COOKING TIP: Want to take some of the "bite" out of those onions? Slice them and place them in a colander and give them a good rinse before adding them to the salad.

SERVING TIP: Try substituting warmed naan or pita for the tortillas for a fun twist.

BEEF RECIPES

Beef is kind of a luxury item our house. While we don't eat it often, we do enjoy it, especially grilled. These beef taco recipes are a collection inspired by flavors from my childhood and flavors inspired by my life here in Chicago. So go fire up your grill and get ready to enjoy some delicious tacos!

BBQ Skirt Steak Tacos

SERVINGS: 4

I don't cook steak that much, but I love a good, well-seasoned and grilled skirt steak. This one starts with a delicious rub made with plenty of spice and a hint of sweetness. It only seemed right to pair it with a fresh cabbage and carrot slaw, don't you think?

For the rub:

2 teaspoons ground cumin

1 teaspoon chili powder

1 tablespoon packed brown sugar

½ teaspoon kosher salt

½ teaspoon Hungarian paprika

¼ teaspoon ground cloves

1 pound skirt steak, trimmed

For the slaw:

2 tablespoons plain Greek yogurt

1 teaspoon apple cider vinegar

1 tablespoon fresh orange juice

2 medium carrots, shredded

2 cups shredded green cabbage

2 green onions, thinly sliced

⅛ teaspoon kosher salt

For the tacos:

8 flour tortillas, warmed

For the rub:

In a small bowl combine the cumin, chili powder, brown sugar, salt, paprika, and cloves. Rub steak all over with the spice mixture and let sit for 30 minutes or up to 1 hour in the fridge.

For the slaw:

Combine the yogurt, apple cider vinegar, and orange juice in a medium mixing bowl. Add the shredded carrot, cabbage, and green onion and toss to coat. Season to taste with salt and black pepper. Cover and refrigerate until ready to serve.

To cook the steak:

Preheat the grill to high heat or set a grill pan over medium-high heat. If using a grill, clean the grill grates and brush them with oil. If using a grill pan, coat pan lightly with oil Once hot, add the steak and cook the steak for 4 to 5 minutes on each side, or until desired degree of doneness.

To make the tacos:

Let steak rest 10 minutes. Slice against the grain and serve in warmed tortillas topped with slaw.

ALTERNATE COOKING INFORMATION: You can prepare this steak in a grill pan, as well. Cook for the same amount of time (adjusting for desired level of doneness) and be sure to coat the pan lightly with vegetable oil before cooking.

Slow Cooker Beef

SERVINGS: 8 TO 12

Remember, the slow cooker is your friend! I love this beef because it's so simple and so flavorful. Plus, it keeps really well in the freezer. That means you can grab it whenever nights get crazy and you need food fast.

For the beef:

1 (2- to 3-pound) boneless beef chuck roast, cut into 4 or 5 large chunks

½ ounce dried mushrooms (porcini or other)

2 tablespoons tomato paste

2 tablespoons Worcestershire sauce

1 teaspoon freshly ground black pepper

1 teaspoon kosher salt

1 teaspoon water

2 garlic cloves, minced

1½ cups low-sodium beef broth or water

For the tacos:

8 to 12 corn or flour tortillas, warmed

Toppings: shredded cabbage, fresh cilantro, pico de gallo, guacamole, etc.

To prepare the rub:

Crush mushrooms to a powder by pulsing in a spice or coffee grinder or finely chop with a knife. Transfer to a small mixing bowl and add the tomato paste, Worcestershire sauce, black pepper, salt, garlic and 1 teaspoon water.

To cook the beef:

Rub the mushroom mixture all over beef, then place in a slow cooker. Add the broth and cook on low for 8 to 10 hours.

To make the tacos:

Remove beef from the slow cooker and chop or shred using two forks. Mix in cooking liquid for added moisture, if desired. Season with additional salt as needed. Serve on warmed tortillas along with your favorite fixings. Or use in any of the recipes below where cooked beef is called for.

RECIPE NOTE: You'll find this recipe throughout the book for use in other recipes! That's why the flavor is mild.

SAVING TIP: Beef can be stored in an air-tight container up to four days in the refrigerator or up to six months in the freezer.

Slow Cooker Beef Fajita Tacos

SERVINGS: 4

When I was growing up, fajitas were SUPER popular. Everyone had to order them because that sizzling plate of food was just "so cool." Well, I still think it's a pretty cool dish myself, so I turned it into a taco! I love using a bunch of bell peppers here and then using that Slow Cooker Beef (see page 86) to help it come together quickly!

For the vegetables:

2 teaspoons extra-virgin olive oil

1 yellow onion, thinly sliced

1 red bell pepper, thinly sliced

1 green bell pepper, thinly sliced

½ jalapeño, thinly sliced (optional)

1 clove garlic, minced

1 teaspoon ground cumin

1 teaspoon chili powder

¼ teaspoon kosher salt

3 tablespoons fresh lime juice

For the tacos:

8 tortillas or other "holder"

2 cups Slow Cooker Beef (see page 86) or any cooked beef

Toppings: salsa, sour cream and diced avocado for serving

To cook the vegetables:

Set a large skillet over medium-high heat and add the oil. Once hot, add the onion, bell peppers, and jalapeño, if using. Cook, stirring often until tender, about 8 minutes. Add the garlic, cumin, chili powder, and salt and cook 1 more minute. Remove from heat and toss the vegetables with the salt and lime juice.

To make the tacos:

Divide the warmed beef among the tortillas and top with vegetables. Garnish with salsa, sour cream and avocado.

COOKING TIP: If you don't have time to make the Slow Cooker Beef, feel free to buy a pound or so of skirt or flank steak at the grocery store. The easiest way to prepare it is to season with a little salt and pepper and broil it for about 4 to 6 minutes on each side. Better yet, if you've got the time, place it in a marinade for about 1 hour before cooking. A marinade could something as simple as oil, garlic, and low-sodium soy sauce. Keep it easy!

Ropa Vieja Tacos

SERVINGS: 4

Capers and olives! Oh my! I do love this Cuban dish, and this recipe has so much rich tomato flavor that really comes alive with those capers and olives! And the longer it all simmers, the better it tastes, trust me!

For the Ropa Vieja:

1 tablespoon extra-virgin olive oil

1 yellow onion, sliced

1 green bell pepper, sliced

1 red bell pepper, sliced

2 garlic cloves, minced

1 teaspoon ground cumin

1 tablespoon tomato paste

1 (8-ounce) can tomato sauce

½ cup green olives, halved and pitted

2 tablespoons capers, rinsed

1 tablespoon red wine vinegar

1 to 1½ cups Slow Cooker Beef (see page 86) or other cooked beef (such as flank steak)

Kosher salt

For the tacos:

8 flour tortillas, warmed

½ cup cilantro, roughly chopped

To make the Ropa Vieja:

Heat the oil in a large skillet over medium heat. Once hot, add the onion and bell peppers. Cook, stirring frequently, until softened, about 10 minutes. Add the garlic and cumin and cook 1 minute. Stir in the tomato paste and cook 1 minute. Add the tomato sauce and stir. Cover, reduce heat to a simmer, and cook for at least 30 minutes and up to 45 minutes to let flavors develop. During the last 5 minutes of cooking, add the olives, capers, red wine vinegar, and beef. Season, to taste, with salt.

To make the tacos:

Serve beef mixture in warmed tortillas. Garnish with cilantro.

RECIPE NOTE: No beef? No problem! Sub in black beans for a vegetarian version!

COOKING TIP: Not using the Slow Cooker Beef? Substitute with 1 to 1½ pounds flank or strip steak. Broil or grill about 5 to 6 minutes on each side. Rest for at least 5 minutes, and then thinly slice against the grain. Add to the Ropa Vieja just before serving.

Slow Cooker Beef Tacos with Pico De Gallo

SERVINGS: 4

A fresh Pico de Gallo makes me so incredibly happy. The ingredients—tomatoes, onion, cilantro, garlic, jalapeño and lime juice—are so simple, but pure perfection! It's a light and refreshing addition to these beefy tacos!

For the pico:

4 to 5 Roma tomatoes

¼ cup chopped white or red onion

½ cup packed cilantro, chopped

1 clove garlic, minced

1 tablespoon chopped serrano or jalapeño pepper

1 lime, juiced

¼ teaspoon kosher salt

For the tacos:

2 to 3 cups shredded slow cooker beef (see Slow Cooker Beef, see page 86), warmed

8 flour tortillas, warmed

Toppings: pickled jalapeños, Plain Greek yogurt and crumbled cotija cheese

To make the pico:

Cut the tomatoes in half and remove and discard the seeds. Chop the tomatoes, then add them along with the onion, cilantro, garlic, serrano pepper, and lime juice to a medium bowl. Mix to combine, adding salt to taste.

To make the tacos:

Serve the beef in warmed tortillas. Top with pico de gallo, pickled jalapeños, yogurt, and cheese.

GROCERY TIP: I love super spicy pickled jalapeños. You can find them in the ethnic food aisle, usually in a can or jar.

SERVING TIP: There's always room for more vegetables! Buy a bag of coleslaw mix and dress it with Creamy Cilantro Dressing (see page 225).

Beef and Broccoli Stir Fry Tacos

SERVINGS: 4

For the sauce:

¼ cup orange marmalade

½ teaspoon crushed red pepper

2 tablespoons fresh lime juice

2 tablespoons low-sodium soy sauce

1 tablespoon cornstarch

1 tablespoon water

For the stir fry:

1 tablespoon vegetable oil

1 pound sirloin steak, trimmed and cut into thin slices

4 cups broccoli florets

1 red bell pepper, cut into large chunks

2 cloves garlic, minced

1 tablespoon minced fresh ginger

3 green onions, white and light green parts only, thinly sliced (reserve 1 to 2 tablespoons for garnish)

1 tablespoon fresh lime juice

For the tacos:

8 hard taco shells, warmed

1 tablespoon sesame seeds, toasted

When I was working in kitchens, stir fries were our go-to meal. Why? Because we knew how to take food scraps and make them delicious! I love stir fries because of their versatility—kind of like tacos!

To make the sauce:

In a small mixing bowl, whisk together the marmalade, crushed red pepper, lime juice, soy sauce, cornstarch, and water.

To cook the stir fry:

Heat the oil in a wok or large, heavy nonstick skillet (or cast-iron pan) over high heat. Add the beef and cook, stirring constantly, until beef is lightly cooked, about 3 minutes. Remove and keep warm. Add broccoli and pepper to the hot pan and cook until crisp tender, about 5 minutes. Stir in the garlic, ginger, and green onions, cook 1 minute. Stir the sauce then add it to the skillet and cook 1 additional minute, or until thickened. Stir in beef, remove from the heat, and add the remaining lime juice.

To make the tacos:

Serve the stir fry in warmed taco shells. Garnish with toasted sesame seeds and green onions.

PREP TIP: Make your life easier when it comes to slicing! Chill that beef in the freezer for about 1 hour before slicing. The partially-frozen beef will be much easier to cut!

COOKING TIP: If florets are large, I recommend cutting them into bite-size pieces. This makes them easier to eat when placed inside that taco shell!

Korean BBQ Beef Tacos

SERVINGS: 4

Have you had Korean BBQ? It's out of this world! I wanted to recreate the delicious food I've experienced and turn it into a taco. This recipe is my homage to Korean BBQ.

For the marinade:

2 cloves garlic, minced

2 tablespoons sesame oil

2 tablespoons vegetable oil

3 tablespoons honey

¼ cup low-sodium soy sauce

2 green onions, light and green parts only, thinly sliced

¼ cup mirin

½ cup pear juice or pineapple juice

1 pound sirloin steak or beef tenderloin, thinly sliced against the grain

For the tacos:

8 (6-inch) flour tortillas, warmed

Toppings: shredded lettuce or cabbage, shredded carrots, kimchi

Special equipment: 10 to 12 wooden skewers, soaked in water for 30 minutes

To make the marinade:

Add the first 8 ingredients to a medium bowl and whisk to combine. Reserve ½ cup. Transfer the remaining marinade to a gallon-size, sealable plastic bag. Add the beef, press out any excess air from the bag, then seal and turn to coat. Marinate for at least 2 hours and up to 12 hours in the refrigerator.

To cook the beef:

Preheat the grill to medium-high heat or set a grill pan over medium-high heat. If using the grill, clean the grill grates and brush them with oil. If using a grill pan, coat pan lightly with oil. Remove beef from the marinade and pat dry; discard the marinade. Thread beef onto soaked skewers then grill 2 to 3 minutes on each side, or until desired degree of doneness.

To make the tacos:

Remove beef from skewers and serve family style with warmed tortillas, shredded lettuce, shredded carrots, and kimchi. Use extra reserved marinade for serving.

PREP TIP: To make slicing the beef easier, freeze it for at least 1 hour and up to 2 hours.

RECIPE NOTE: If you can't find mirin, you can substitute it in this recipe with 1½ teaspoons sugar mixed with ¼ cup rice vinegar.

COOKING TIP: This recipe can also be prepared without using skewers—the skewers simply make it easier to handle the beef while it's on the hot grill.

Hamburger Tacos

SERVINGS: 4

If you have kids, they'll love this recipe. Because what's better than a hamburger? A hamburger in a taco, that's what! They'll love filling tortillas with hamburger and topping with their favorite condiments and accoutrement.

For the hamburger filling:

1 pound 85% lean ground beef

½ medium yellow onion, finely chopped

1 garlic clove, minced

1 tablespoon Worcestershire sauce

½ cup shredded cheddar cheese

For the tacos:

8 (6-inch) corn or flour tortillas, warmed

Toppings: chopped, ripe tomato, shredded lettuce, thinly sliced or finely chopped red or white onion, pickle slices, ketchup and mustard

To cook the hamburger filling:

Set a large skillet over medium-high heat. Add the ground beef and cook, stirring to crumble, until browned, about 5 to 8 minutes. Drain most of the fat, leaving about a teaspoon, then add the onion and garlic and cook 4 to 5 minutes, covered, stirring occasionally, until slightly softened. Reduce heat to medium low and stir in the Worcestershire sauce, scraping any bits off the bottom of the pan. Cook 1 minute.

Remove pan from the heat, sprinkle cheese over the top, and cover with a piece of foil. Let "steam" about 5 minutes, or until cheese is melted.

To make the tacos:

Serve hamburger mixture in warmed tortillas and garnish with your favorite toppings.

RECIPE NOTE: This recipe is also great with other ground meats. Try ground turkey, chicken, or even bison.

SERVING TIP: These are also delicious served in a crunchy hard taco shell!

Red Curry Flank Steak Tacos

SERVINGS: 4

Flank steak is a lean, delicious choice when it comes to beef. It's also simple to cook. This recipe uses red curry paste, an ingredient that could be hard to find. Look for it in the ethnic aisle in your grocery store.

1 pound flank steak

For the marinade:

2 cloves garlic, minced

1 tablespoon red curry paste

1 tablespoon fresh ginger, peeled and minced

2 tablespoons fresh lime juice

1 tablespoon packed brown sugar

¼ cup light coconut milk

1 teaspoon kosher salt

For the apple topping:

2 small crisp, sweet apples such as Fuji or gala, cored and cut into matchstick strips

½ cup lightly packed cilantro leaves

½ cup thinly sliced red onion

2 tablespoons fresh lime juice

For the tacos:

8 hard taco shells, warmed

Plain Greek yogurt, for serving

To prepare the steak:

Using a sharp knife, make cross hatch marks on the steak, about ¼ inch deep, on each side.

Combine the marinade ingredients in a large, shallow dish. Add the steak and rub marinade all over. Cover and refrigerate for at least 1 hour and up to 12 hours.

To cook the steak:

Position the oven rack 5 to 6 inches from the heating element and preheat the broiler. Line a broiler pan with foil. Remove steak from marinade and pat dry; discard marinade. Place steak on prepared pan. Broil 4 to 5 minutes per side, or until desired degree of doneness. Rest for 5 minutes before slicing thinly against the grain.

While steak is resting, prepare the topping:

To a medium bowl, add the apple, cilantro, and red onion. Toss with the lime juice and a pinch of salt, if desired.

To make the tacos:

Serve steak in warmed taco shells and garnish with apple topping and a dollop of yogurt.

RECIPE NOTE: Fresh ginger wins over powdered for this recipe. Find it in the produce section of your grocery store. Break off a hunk of the root if you only want a small piece.

COOKING TIP: What does cutting against the grain mean? Look at your steak and identify the striations (or lines on it). Once you've ID'd them, notice which direction they are running—that's the "grain." When you slice, slice perpendicular to that grain.

Slow Cooker Beef Tacos with Caramelized Onions and Horseradish Sauce

SERVINGS: 4

For the onions:

2 teaspoons extra-virgin olive oil

1 teaspoon unsalted butter

1 Vidalia or other sweet onion, sliced ⅛-inch thick

For the horseradish sauce:

1 tablespoon prepared horseradish

⅓ cup plain Greek yogurt

1 teaspoon fresh lemon juice

¼ teaspoon freshly ground black pepper

⅛ teaspoon kosher salt

For the tacos:

2 cups shredded Slow Cooker Beef (see page 86) or other cooked beef

8 (6-inch) flour tortillas, warmed

4 cups baby arugula

When I was a kid, my mom used to make what she called "flank steak sandwiches." Basically, sliced Italian bread, toasted, then topped with butter, some thinly sliced grilled flank steak, caramelized onions, and a sour cream horseradish sauce. It was dreamy. These tacos are based on that fabulous childhood meal.

To cook the onions:

Place olive oil and butter in a medium non-stick skillet and set over medium heat. Once butter has melted, add the onion and cook 5 minutes, stirring often. Reduce heat to low, cover, and cook an additional 30, minutes, stirring occasionally.

To make the horseradish sauce:

In a bowl, combine the horseradish, yogurt, lemon juice, black pepper, and salt.

To make the tacos:

Serve beef in warmed tortillas and top with horseradish sauce, onions, and arugula.

GROCERY TIP: Can't find Vidalia onions? That's okay, substitute with white or yellow onion.

PORK RECIPES

There are so many cuts of pork, and many of them work so well with tacos! I've got a mix of everything in this pork section, from a slow cooker Pork Tinga recipe to super easy Ham and Arugula Tacos, you'll find plenty of variety in here!

Drunken Slow Cooker Pork Tacos

SERVINGS: 6 TO 8

You know what tastes good? Pork that cooks all day in beer. It's a very good thing. After it's done cooking, you'll turn that braising liquid into a super yummy sauce infused with molasses and brown sugar. You're welcome.

For the pork:

1 tablespoon chili powder

3 tablespoons packed light brown sugar

2 cloves garlic, minced

½ teaspoon kosher salt

1 (1½- to 2-pound) pork loin roast, trimmed of excess fat

1 small yellow or white onion, sliced

8 fluid ounces brown ale beer

For the sauce:

2 tablespoons apple cider vinegar

1 tablespoon packed light brown sugar

2 teaspoons molasses

Kosher salt and freshly cracked black pepper

For the tacos:

12 to 16 (6-inch) corn or flour tortillas

Toppings: shredded lettuce, feta or cojita cheese, pickled jalapeños, avocado, guacamole etc.

To cook the pork:

In a small bowl, combine the chili powder, brown sugar, garlic, and salt. Rub seasoning mixture all over pork roast. (If doing this step the night before, place the pork in a rimmed baking dish or rimmed sheet pan, cover, and refrigerate.)

Spread the sliced onions in the bottom of a 6-quart slow cooker. Place pork roast on top of the onions. Pour the beer around the roast. Cover slow cooker with a lid and cook on low for 8 to 10 hours.

To make the sauce:

Carefully remove the braising liquid and place it in a skillet set over medium-high heat along with the remaining brown sugar and molasses. Cook until mixture is slightly thickened and syrupy, about 10 to 12 minutes.

While braising liquid is reducing, shred the pork:

Using two forks, pull pork apart inside the slow cooker. Add the reduced braising liquid and the apple cider vinegar. Season with salt and pepper, if desired.

To make the tacos:

Serve pork on warmed tortillas with toppings of your choice such as shredded lettuce, feta cheese, pickled jalapeños, etc.

RECIPE NOTE: If you don't have any molasses, you can substitute with an equal amount of honey or maple syrup.

Pork Tinga Slow Cooker Tacos

SERVINGS: 6 TO 8 (MAKES ABOUT 4 CUPS COOKED PORK)

I recently went to a local Mexican restaurant that served a chicken tinga taco, and it made me SO HAPPY. Of course I had to come home and immediately try to recreate it. I came pretty darn close with this one. Instead of chicken, I swapped in pork for a fun twist. And I like to keep the toppings simple because the sauce it cooks in tastes so good!

For the pork:

1 tablespoon vegetable oil

1 large yellow onion, chopped

1 large tomato, chopped

1 (7-ounce) can tomatillo salsa (or about 1 cup tomatillo salsa)

2 cloves garlic, minced

1 chipotle chile canned in adobo

1 tablespoon adobo sauce (from canned chipotle chiles)

¼ cup low-sodium chicken broth or water

1 (2- to 2½-pound) boneless pork loin roast

For the tacos:

12 (6-inch) corn tortillas, warmed

Toppings: shredded lettuce, such as romaine, shredded red or green cabbage, thinly sliced radish, crumbled cotija cheese, sliced or diced avocado

To make the sauce:

Set a large skillet over medium heat and add the oil. Once hot, add the onion and tomatoes and cook, stirring frequently, for 5 minutes. Add the tomatillo salsa and garlic, cook 1 more minute. Stir in the chipotle and adobo and remove from the heat. Allow to cool slightly, then transfer to a blender along with the broth or water and carefully puree until smooth (alternatively, you can use an immersion blender to puree).

To cook the pork:

Place pork in the bottom of a 5- to 6-quart slow cooker. Pour pureed sauce over the pork, then cover with a lid and cook on low for 8 to 9 hours.

To shred the pork:

Using two forks, shred the pork (this can be done inside the slow cooker). Toss with the sauce and cook an additional 10 to 15 minutes to meld flavors. Season to taste with salt and pepper.

To make the tacos:

Serve pork in warmed tortillas, then top with shredded lettuce, shredded cabbage, thinly sliced radish, and cotija cheese.

RECIPE NOTE: I know it seems like a pain to cook something before slow cooking it, but I promise this is worth it!

SERVING TIP: Pile the veggies on for these tacos! The crunchier, the better!

Ham and Arugula Taco

SERVINGS: 4

If you haven't noticed, I really like arugula. Something about its peppery brightness is so delightful. I think it's great when paired with ham and stone-ground mustard. To cut that bitterness and tanginess, I add some sliced apple for just a hint of sweetness.

For the tacos:

8 (6-inch) corn tortillas

8 ounces baked ham, thinly sliced

1 small red onion, thinly sliced

¾ cup shredded sharp cheddar cheese

For the arugula salad:

1 tablespoon whole grain mustard

1 teaspoon red wine vinegar

1 teaspoon honey

2 tablespoons extra-virgin olive oil

4 cups baby arugula

For serving:

1 Fuji apple, sliced into strips

To prepare the tacos:

Preheat the oven to 400°F and line a baking sheet with foil.

Place tortillas on the prepared pan and top each with some of the ham, onion, and cheese. Leave flat and bake for 8 to 10 minutes, checking after 8 minutes, until cheese is melted.

While tacos are baking, make the arugula salad: In a medium mixing bowl, whisk together the mustard, vinegar, honey, and olive oil. Add the arugula and toss to coat.

To make the tacos:

Remove the tacos from the oven and top each with some of the arugula mixture and apples slices. Fold up and serve immediately.

RECIPE NOTE: Arugula not your thing? Replace it with spinach!

COOKING TIP: You can slice the apple however you want. I like to slice them into little matchstick strips so that I get plenty of apple goodness in every bite!

Pork Sausage and Sauerkraut Tacos with Apple Slaw

SERVINGS: 4

Remember when I said I was from Indiana? Well, that means I automatically like pork and pork products, or so I've been told. And with a strong German heritage, it's no surprise that I do like a good pork sausage paired with sauerkraut! So, of course I had to turn THAT into a taco. And to add a bit of freshness to what could've been a pretty heavy taco, I added a simple apple slaw. It's a nice, balanced approach to honor my Hoosier roots.

For the sausage:

2 teaspoons extra-virgin olive oil

12 ounces (about 4 links) pork sausage, cut into ½-inch slices

1 cup sauerkraut

8 fluid ounces German-style beer, such as Hefeweizen

For the apple slaw:

1 teaspoon whole grain mustard

Pinch ground cloves

1 tablespoon fresh lemon juice

1 tablespoon apple cider vinegar

1 tablespoon extra-virgin olive oil

1 Granny Smith apple, thinly sliced into sticks

¼ cup thinly sliced red onion

For the tacos:

8 (6-inch) flour tortillas, warmed

To cook the sausage:

Heat the oil in a large skillet over medium heat. Once hot, add the sausage and cook, stirring often, until browned, about 4–5 minutes. Add the sauerkraut and beer and cook, partially covered, until most of the liquid has cooked off, about 15 minutes.

To make the apple slaw:

In a medium bowl, whisk together the mustard, cloves, lemon juice, and apple cider vinegar. Add the oil and whisk until combined. Add the apple and red onion and toss. Season to taste with salt and black pepper.

To make the tacos:

Serve sausage and sauerkraut in warmed tortillas and top with slaw.

RECIPE NOTE: I like the tartness of a Granny Smith apple for this slaw, but feel free to experiment and try different crisp apples in its place.

RECIPE NOTE: Whole grain mustard is not the same as yellow, brown, or Dijon mustard. Unlike those mustards, whole grain mustard contains partially ground mustard seeds, leaving more texture and heat than other mustards.

Apricot Maple Pork Tenderloin Tacos with Pickled Pineapple

SERVINGS: 4

For the pickled pineapple:

2 cups cubed, fresh pineapple

½ cup water

½ cup pineapple juice

⅓ cup white vinegar

3 whole black peppercorns

3 whole cloves

For the pork:

¼ teaspoon kosher salt

¼ teaspoon freshly ground black pepper

2 teaspoons chili powder

2 teaspoons ground cumin

¼ cup maple syrup

2 tablespoons apricot jam or jelly

1 (1- to 1 ¼-pound) pork tenderloin, trimmed of fat and silver-skin

1 tablespoon extra-virgin olive oil

For the tacos:

8 (6-inch) corn tortillas, warmed

2 cups shredded green or purple cabbage

1 lime, cut into wedges

Pickled pineapple? Yes! You can pickle pineapple and it's delicious! Pineapple and pork are a perfect pairing and make for an excellent taco.

To make the pickled pineapple:

Place the pineapple in a medium non-reactive bowl (such as glass or stainless steel). Bring water, pineapple juice, vinegar, peppercorns, and cloves to a boil in a non-reactive pot. Pour mixture over the pineapple, and then set aside to cool. Once mixture has cooled, cover and refrigerate for at least 30 minutes.

To cook the pork loin:

Preheat the oven to 400°F. In a small bowl, combine the salt, pepper, chili powder, and cumin. Pat pork loin dry and pat seasoning onto all sides. To the now-empty bowl, combine the maple syrup with the apricot jam; set aside.

Heat the oil a heavy oven-proof skillet, such as cast-iron, over medium-high heat. Once hot, add the pork to the pan and cook about 2 to 3 minutes per side, until browned. Move the pork to the oven and cook for 6 minutes. Carefully drizzle half of the maple mixture over the top of the loin, flip over, and then add the remaining maple mixture and cook an additional 6 to 8 minutes, until internal temperature reaches a minimum of 145°F in the thickest part of the pork. Remove pork from the skillet, cover with foil, and let rest 5 minutes.

To make the tacos:

Slice the pork thinly and serve on warmed tortillas. Drizzle with remaining maple-apricot from the pan and top with pickled pineapple and cabbage. Serve with a lime wedge.

FISH AND SEAFOOD RECIPES

I cannot get enough fish these days. I love how satisfying it is without being "heavy." Plus, there are so many different kinds, which makes it fun to experiment with. In this chapter, you'll see how much fun fish can be! I've got all kinds of fish and seafood recipes for you to try.

Blackened Fish Tacos with Caper Remoulade

SERVINGS: 4

I've always been fascinated with blackening seasoning. I love the fiery flavor and how great it tastes when paired with something creamy to balance it. That's why I made a slightly salty, definitely creamy remoulade sauce to manage all of that heat!

For the sauce:

2 tablespoons plain Greek yogurt

3 tablespoons extra-virgin olive oil mayonnaise or other mayonnaise

2 tablespoons minced sweet pickle

1 tablespoon capers, rinsed and minced

1 teaspoon Dijon mustard

1 teaspoon fresh lemon juice

For the blackening rub and fish:

1 teaspoon ground smoked paprika

1 teaspoon garlic powder

1 teaspoon onion powder

⅛ to ¼ teaspoon cayenne pepper

1 teaspoon dried thyme leaves

¼ teaspoon kosher salt

½ teaspoon freshly ground black pepper

To make the sauce:

In a small bowl, combine the yogurt, mayonnaise, pickle, capers, mustard, and lemon juice. Set aside or refrigerate until ready to serve.

To prepare the rub/fish:

Combine the spices in a small bowl. Pat fish dry, then press spice mixture evenly to cover each fish fillet.

To cook the fish:

Heat the oil in a cast iron pan or other heavy non-stick pan over medium-high heat until hot. Add the fish to the pan and cook 3 minutes. Flip and cook an additional 3 to 4 minutes or until fish is cooked and flakes easily with a fork and internal temperature reaches 145°F. Remove from heat and squeeze with fresh lemon juice.

To make the tacos:

Serve the fish in the warmed naan topped with sauce, shredded cabbage, and corn.

1 pound cod fillets

2 teaspoons vegetable oil

1 to 2 teaspoons fresh lemon juice

For the tacos:

4 ounces cabbage, shredded

1 cup sweet corn, cooked

4 whole wheat naan, warmed, then sliced in half vertically.

GROCERY TIP: Any mild whitefish will work here—try cod, haddock, catfish, bass, or snapper.

RECIPE NOTE: Don't be scared by the number of ingredients here. It's likely you have many of them already on hand!

Chipotle Fish Tacos with Avocado Pineapple Salsa

SERVINGS: 4

Looking for a simple weeknight meal? This is the one for you! This fish cooks FAST! And the avocado and pineapple salsa can easily be made while your fish is cooking. Then pat yourself on the back, because even though you were time-strapped, you still made dinner!

For the fish:

1 tablespoon extra-virgin olive oil

1 chipotle chile canned in adobo, roughly chopped

2 teaspoons adobo sauce

2 teaspoons maple syrup

4 (4- to 5-ounce) tilapia fillets

¼ teaspoon kosher salt

For the salsa:

1 cup fresh or canned pineapple, chopped

½ small red onion, chopped

¼ cup fresh cilantro, chopped

½ large red bell pepper, diced

1 avocado, seeded and diced

Juice and zest of 1 lime

¼ teaspoon kosher salt

For the tacos:

8 (6-inch) flour tortillas, warmed or large lettuce leaves, such as romaine

To cook the fish:

Position the oven rack about 5 to 6 inches away from the heating element and preheat the broiler. Line a rimmed baking sheet or broiler pan with foil and coat with non-stick cooking spray.

In a small bowl, combine the oil, chipotle, adobo, and maple syrup. Place the fish on a prepared pan and season with salt. Spread mixture over non-skinned sides of the fillets and place on the prepared pan. Broil fish until the internal temperature reaches 145°F or until fish flakes easily with a fork, about 5 to 8 minutes total.

While fish is cooking, make the salsa:

To a medium bowl, add the pineapple, red onion, cilantro, bell pepper, avocado, lime juice, and salt. Stir gently to combine. Set aside.

To make the tacos:

Pull tilapia apart gently using forks and add to warmed tortillas. Top with pineapple salsa and enjoy!

GROCERY TIP: If buying canned pineapple, choose the one packed in its own juices. The other versions are too cloyingly sweet and not appropriate for this recipe.

INGREDIENT TIP: What is adobo sauce? It's the delicious sauce made with chiles and other seasonings that comes with canned chipotles. It's magical!

Coconut Fish Tacos with Sweet Chili Sauce

SERVINGS: 4

I love coconut shrimp at restaurants. Yes, I know that it's deep fried, but it just tastes so good. But, let's get real; it does NOT leave me feeling so good. So, that's why I created this recipe. Instead of shrimp, I use fish, and instead of frying, I bake the fish. The result is something just as good, if not better, than the restaurant versions!

For the sweet chili sauce:

2 tablespoons rice wine vinegar

2 tablespoons white vinegar

½ cup + 1 tablespoon water, divided

2 cloves garlic, finely chopped

3 tablespoons honey

¼ teaspoon crushed red pepper

1 tablespoon corn starch

For the fish:

4 (4- to 5-ounce) tilapia fillets

¼ cup all-purpose flour

1 cup lite coconut milk

1 cup panko bread crumbs

½ cup coconut flakes, chopped

½ teaspoon kosher salt

For the tacos:

8 (6-inch) corn tortillas, warmed

Toppings: red onion, thinly sliced, cabbage, thinly sliced, cilantro leaves

To make the sweet chili sauce:

In a small saucepan, combine the vinegars, ½ cup water, garlic, honey, and crushed red pepper. Set the pan over medium heat and bring to a boil. Reduce the heat and simmer 5 minutes. Mix the remaining 1 tablespoon water with the cornstarch. Whisk into sauce and cook 1 minute or until thickened. Set aside while you cook the fish.

To cook the fish:

Preheat the oven to 400°F and line a large baking sheet with foil. Coat the foil with non-stick cooking spray.

Place the flour in a shallow dish, the coconut milk in another shallow dish, and combine the panko bread crumbs with the coconut flakes in a separate shallow dish.

Season the fish with salt, then dredge each piece, one at a time, in the flour mixture, dip into the coconut milk, and then coat with the breadcrumb mixture. Place fish on the prepared pan and bake, turning once, for 15 to 20 minutes or until internal temperature reaches 145°F.

To make the tacos:

Serve fish on warmed tortillas, drizzle with chili sauce, and garnish with onion, cabbage, and cilantro.

GROCERY TIP: Make sure you buy unsweetened coconut flakes for this recipe. If you can't find flakes, substitute with unsweetened, shredded coconut.

GROCERY TIP: If you can find them, use whole wheat panko for a whole grain kick!

Brown Sugar Chili Salmon Tacos

SERVINGS: 4

One of the meals I used to make for my husband all of the time was a maple chili salmon dish. I loved how simple yet flavorful it was. This recipe is a riff on that family favorite. But this time, I've turned it into a taco and paired it with creamy guacamole and crunchy cabbage!

For the salmon:

1 to 2 teaspoons chili powder

1 tablespoon packed light brown sugar

1 teaspoon ground cumin

2 teaspoons extra-virgin olive oil

¼ teaspoon kosher salt

1 (1 pound) skin-on, wild salmon fillet

For the guacamole topping:

1 ripe avocado

2 teaspoons fresh lime juice

¼ teaspoon kosher salt

½ jalapeño, diced

1 scallion, white and light green parts only, thinly sliced

1 tablespoon fresh lime juice

For serving:

8 (6-inch) corn or flour tortillas, warmed

2 to 3 cups shredded green cabbage

To cook the salmon:

Position the oven rack about 5 to 6 inches from the heating element and preheat the broiler. Line a rimmed baking sheet or broiler pan with foil and coat with nonstick cooking spray.

In a small bowl, combine the chili powder, brown sugar, cumin, and oil.

Place the salmon on the prepared pan, skin-side down. Sprinkle with salt then place in the oven and broil for 5 minutes. Remove from the oven and spread brown sugar mixture over the salmon, then cook an additional 2 to 3 minutes, or until fish flakes easily with a fork and internal temperature reaches 145°F.

While salmon is cooking, prepare the guacamole:

Remove the avocado seed and scoop the avocado flesh out of the skin into a medium bowl. Mash with a fork then add the salt, jalapeño, scallion, and lime juice. Stir to combine.

To make the tacos:

Using a fork, break salmon into large pieces. Portion cooked salmon among tortillas and top with guacamole and cabbage.

KITCHEN TIP: Go with fresh! In all of my recipes, wherever I call for citrus juice, I mean fresh citrus juice. While the jarred versions are handy, their taste is never quite the same as that from fresh citrus.

Salmon Tacos with Sesame Salad

SERVINGS: 4

Canned salmon can be a real life saver when you're hungry. I love it tossed with vibrant Asian flavors like miso and ginger, and it tastes great with a healthy dose of Sesame Salad. And I advise buying the good canned salmon, because you're worth it!

For the salmon salad:

1 tablespoon white miso (shiro)

1 tablespoon minced fresh ginger

1 clove garlic, minced

2 green onions, sliced, plus extra for garnish

2 teaspoons sesame oil

2 tablespoons fresh lime juice

2 (6-ounce) cans sockeye salmon

For the sesame salad:

8 radishes, thinly sliced

1 medium carrot, shredded

1 bell pepper (red, yellow or orange), thinly sliced

1 teaspoon sesame oil

1 tablespoon rice wine vinegar

1 teaspoon white sesame seeds

For the tacos:

8 hard taco shells, warmed

To make the salmon salad:

To a medium bowl, add the miso, ginger, garlic, onions, sesame oil, and lime juice. Whisk to combine then gently fold in flaked, canned salmon.

To make the salad topping:

In a separate medium bowl, combine the radish, carrot, and bell pepper. Toss with the sesame oil, vinegar and sesame seeds.

To make the tacos:

Serve salmon salad mixture in taco shells and top with sesame salad. Garnish with extra green onion, if desired.

PREP TIP: Have a little extra time? Go ahead and toast those sesame seeds before you add them to the salad. Simply place them in a nonstick pan and cook over medium low heat, stirring occasionally, until lightly browned and toasted, about 1 minute.

RECIPE NOTE: If desired, you can swap in cooked, fresh salmon for the canned salmon.

Bistro Tuna Tacos

SERVINGS: 4

I grew up on the traditional creamy tuna salad, but sometimes I want something a little lighter. That means no mayo, please. Enter this delightful tuna salad taco made with salty cornichons, stone ground mustard, and white wine vinegar.

For the tuna:

1 tablespoon + 1 teaspoon stone ground mustard

1 tablespoon + 1 teaspoon white wine vinegar

2 tablespoons extra-virgin olive oil

2 tablespoons minced red onion

6 small cornichons, chopped

2 (5-ounce) cans chunk light tuna, packed in water, drained

For the tacos:

8 hard taco shells or 8 large lettuce leaves

4 cups baby arugula

1 lemon, cut into wedges

To make the tuna:

In the bottom of a bowl, whisk together the mustard, vinegar, and olive oil. Add the onion and cornichons and stir to combine. Flake the tuna into the bowl and mix gently until well-coated in dressing.

To make the tacos:

Serve tuna in taco shells or lettuce leaves and top with arugula. Serve with a lemon wedge.

RECIPE NOTE: Canned tuna not your thing? Substitute with cooked, fresh tuna instead!

RECIPE NOTE: No cornichons? No problem! Substitute the cornichons with 2 tablespoons of chopped dill pickle.

SERVING TIP: If you're going sans taco shell and using lettuce, I recommend using large leaves of romaine or leaf lettuce.

Grilled Coriander Shrimp Tacos

SERVINGS: 4

For the shrimp:

2 teaspoons ground coriander

2 cloves garlic, smashed

¼ cup vegetable oil

2 tablespoons fresh lime juice

12 ounces large uncooked shrimp, peeled and deveined

For the salsa:

1 (15-ounce) can black beans, drained and rinsed

1 cup cooked sweet corn, fresh or thawed from frozen (or grilled)

½ cup lightly packed fresh cilantro, chopped

½ small jalapeño, thinly sliced

1 tablespoon fresh lime juice

Kosher salt

For the lime crema:

½ cup plain Greek yogurt

2 tablespoons fresh lime juice

⅛ teaspoon ground coriander

For the tacos:

8 (6-inch) flour tortillas or yogurt flatbreads

Special equipment: four wooden skewers, soaked in water for 30 minutes

Have you experimented with coriander at all? It's fabulous! And did you know that it's actually the seed of the cilantro plant? That's right, so if you grow your own cilantro, be sure to save those seeds! Dry them out and then enjoy them in dishes just like this one!

To prepare the shrimp:

Add the coriander, garlic, vegetable oil, and lime juice to a gallon-size, sealable plastic bag. Seal and shake to combine. Add shrimp, press out any excess air from the bag, then reseal and turn to coat. Marinate shrimp for up to 30 minutes in the refrigerator.

To make the salsa:

Combine the black beans, corn, cilantro, jalapeño, and lime juice in a bowl. Season with salt and pepper, to taste.

For the lime crema:

In a small bowl, whisk together the yogurt, lime juice, and coriander. Set aside.

To cook the shrimp:

Preheat the grill to medium-high heat or set a grill pan over medium-high heat. If using a grill, clean the grill grates and brush them with oil. If using a grill pan, coat pan lightly with oil. Remove shrimp from the marinade and pat dry; discard marinade. Thread shrimp on skewers. Grill about 4 minutes on each side, or until shrimp is cooked through.

To make the tacos:

Remove shrimp from skewers and serve on warmed tortillas with salsa and crema.

COOKING TIP: You can skip the skewers if you'd like, but they do make turning and cooking the shrimp easier.

Thai Peanut Shrimp Tacos

SERVINGS: 4

For the cilantro oil:

1 cup lightly packed cilantro leaves and stems, plus more for garnish

3 tablespoons extra-virgin olive oil

1 tablespoon water

1 clove garlic

For the Sriracha peanut sauce:

¼ cup creamy natural peanut butter

1 tablespoon Sriracha

1 teaspoon low-sodium soy sauce

2 tablespoons water

1 tablespoon fresh lime juice

For the shrimp:

1 pound large shrimp, peeled and deveined

¼ teaspoon kosher salt

1 tablespoon vegetable oil

For the tacos:

2 whole wheat naan, warmed and sliced in half vertically

1 cup shredded carrot

1 red bell pepper, sliced

1 to 2 tablespoons chopped peanuts

This dish was originally designed as a pizza! It was so successful that way, that I figured, "Why not turn it into a taco?" And you know what? It worked! I love the spicy peanut sauce, it's something that I make often and keep in my fridge for other meals!

For the cilantro oil:

In a blender or bowl of a small food processor, combine the cilantro, olive oil, water, and garlic. Puree until smooth then transfer to a bowl.

For the Sriracha peanut sauce:

Clean out blender or food processor, then add the peanut butter, Sriracha, soy sauce, water, and lime juice. Puree until smooth. Set aside.

For the shrimp:

Pat the shrimp dry with clean paper towels. Season with salt. Set a large skillet over medium-high heat and add the oil. Once hot, add the shrimp and cook, flipping once halfway through cooking time, for about 5 to 7 minutes, or until shrimp is cooked through.

To make the tacos:

Serve shrimp on warmed naan drizzled with cilantro oil and topped with carrots, peppers, and peanuts. Finish with a drizzle of the peanut sauce.

ALTERNATE COOKING INFORMATION: Want to use the oven instead? Preheat to 400°F and spread shrimp out onto a foil-lined sheet pan that has been sprayed with non-stick cooking spray. Drizzle with olive oil and season with salt and pepper. Cook for about 6 to 8 minutes, or until pink and cooked through.

RECIPE NOTE: I like natural peanut butter for my recipes. The ingredients are simple, just peanuts and sometimes salt. I don't need anything else (like added sugar or oil) in my PB!

SERVING TIP: Want more than one taco per person? Instead of using two whole wheat naan, use four, so that everyone gets two tacos each.

PSF Baja Fish Tacos

SERVINGS: 4

For the Sriracha aioli:

1 tablespoon Sriracha

2 tablespoons plain Greek yogurt

2 tablespoons mayonnaise

1 tablespoon fresh lime juice

For the avocado cilantro sauce:

½ ripe avocado

1 clove garlic

¼ cup cilantro, chopped

1 tablespoon fresh lime juice

2 tablespoons plain Greek yogurt

2 tablespoons water

¼ teaspoon kosher salt

For the fish:

2 teaspoons ground cumin

2 teaspoons chili powder

2 teaspoons packed light brown sugar

¼ teaspoons kosher salt

2 tablespoons + 1 tablespoon extra-virgin olive oil, divided

1 pound skinless cod fillets

For the tacos:

8 (6-inch) corn tortillas, warmed

2 cups shredded cabbage

Exercise has always been a huge part of who I am. There's something magical about getting your heart rate up and feeling those endorphins running. And I'm lucky enough to live in a city with an equally magical place to burn, baby burn. These tacos are for YOU Powersculpt Fitness (aka PSF)! Heather Hughes, the owner and my hero, was the inspiration behind these delightful Baja-inspired fish tacos.

For the Sriracha aioli:

In a small bowl, combine the Sriracha, yogurt, mayonnaise, and lime juice.

For the avocado cilantro sauce:

Place the avocado, garlic, cilantro, lime juice, yogurt, water, and salt in the bowl of a small food processor and blend until smooth.

For the fish:

In a small bowl, mix together the cumin, chili powder, brown sugar, and salt. Stir in 2 tablespoons of olive oil. Rub mixture all over the fish.

Heat the remaining tablespoon of oil in a cast iron pan or other heavy non-stick pan over medium-high heat until hot. Add the fish to the pan and cook 3 minutes. Reduce heat to medium, flip and cook an additional 3 to 4 minutes or until fish is cooked and flakes easily with a fork and internal temperature reaches 145°F.

To make the tacos:

Break fish into large pieces and place on warmed tortillas. Drizzle with Sriracha aioli then top with shredded cabbage and a healthy drizzle of avocado sauce.

. . . continued on next page

GROCERY TIP: You can buy cabbage pre-shredded. Do yourself a favor and buy it to save some time. You can also use a bagged coleslaw mix here.

RECIPE NOTE: Not into mayo? No problem! Omit the mayo and replace with an equal amount of yogurt.

COOKING TIP: If you use frozen fish in this recipe (which you totally can), be sure to thaw thoroughly and pat dry. Soggy fish = yucky fish.

Pan-Seared White Fish Tacos with Lemon Aioli

SERVINGS: 4

For the aioli:

2 tablespoons extra-virgin olive oil mayonnaise

2 tablespoons plain Greek yogurt

2 teaspoons fresh lemon juice

½ teaspoon lemon zest

1 teaspoon Dijon mustard

2 teaspoons capers, rinsed and roughly chopped

1 clove garlic, minced

Freshly ground black pepper

For the fish:

1 tablespoon extra-virgin olive oil

1¼ pounds skinless cod fillets

¼ teaspoon kosher salt

⅛ teaspoon freshly ground black pepper

All-purpose flour, for dusting

For the tacos:

8 (6-inch) flour tortillas, warmed

1 shallot, thinly sliced

4 cups baby arugula

1 lemon, quartered

I've been trying to eat more fish these days—not an easy task when you live in the Midwest, but it can be done! When fresh isn't available, I go with frozen; it's flash frozen on the boat after it's caught, so it's nutritionally comparable to its fresh counterparts. So go ahead, eat more fish!

To make the aioli:

In a small bowl whisk together the mayonnaise, yogurt, lemon juice and zest, mustard, capers, and garlic. Season with black pepper, to taste. Cover and refrigerate until ready to serve.

To cook the fish:

Set a large non-stick pan over medium-high heat and add the oil. Pat the fish dry, then season with salt and pepper. Dust both sides of fish lightly with flour. Add the fish, skinned side up, to the hot pan and cook undisturbed for about 5 minutes. Turn fillets over and cook an additional 4 to 5 minutes, until fish flakes easily with a fork or until internal temperature reaches 145°F.

To make the tacos:

Serve the fish in warmed tortillas and top with aioli, shallot, arugula, and a squeeze of lemon juice.

RECIPE NOTE: I like to use cod for these tacos, but tilapia, haddock, or catfish will work too.

COOKING TIP: For a thicker aioli, use ¼ cup mayonnaise and omit Greek yogurt.

VEGETARIAN RECIPES

Think veggies don't make for good tacos? I totally disagree! In fact, I think veggie tacos are often some of the BEST tacos. That's why I've included fourteen of them in this book. So go ahead, hit that produce aisle hard and prepare yourself for some pretty yummy tacos!

Cumin Chickpea Tacos

SERVINGS: 8

For the salsa:

1 pound tomatillos, skins removed and washed

1 small white onion, chopped

2 cloves garlic, skins removed

2 teaspoons extra-virgin olive oil

½ lime, juiced

¼ cup lightly packed cilantro

For the chickpeas:

1 (15.5-ounce) can chickpeas, drained, rinsed and patted dry

1 tablespoon extra-virgin olive oil

1 teaspoon ground cumin

¼ teaspoon kosher salt

1 teaspoon fresh lime juice

For the cabbage slaw:

¼ cup plain Greek yogurt

Zest and juice of 1 lime

¼ teaspoon kosher salt

½ head purple cabbage, thinly sliced

1 jalapeño, thinly sliced

For the tacos:

16 (6-inch) corn tortillas, warmed

Beans are the best! They're inexpensive, satisfying, and delicious! And I love these tacos because chickpeas just happen to be my favorite bean and cumin just happens to be my favorite spice. You'll never miss the meat in these tacos because of all of the flavor!

For the salsa:

Position oven rack about 6 inches from the heating element and preheat the broiler. Line a rimmed baking sheet or broiler pan with foil and coat with nonstick cooking spray.

Quarter the tomatillos and add them to a bowl along with the onion, garlic, and olive oil. Toss to coat. Spread mixture out onto the prepared baking sheet. Broil 4 minutes, stir, then broil 2 more minutes. Stir again and broil an additional 2 minutes, or until tomatillos and onion are blistered and browned. Remove and cool slightly before transferring to a blender or the bowl of a food processor. Add the lime juice and cilantro and puree until smooth. Season with salt to taste, if desired.

For the chickpeas:

Set a large, non-stick pan over medium-high heat and add the oil. Add the chickpeas and cook, stirring often, until toasted, about 2 to 3 minutes. Add the cumin and cook 1 more minute. Remove from heat and stir in the salt and lime juice.

For the cabbage slaw:

Combine the yogurt, lime juice, zest, and salt in the bottom of a mixing bowl. Add the cabbage and jalapeño and toss to combine.

. . . continued on next page

To make the tacos:

Serve chickpeas in warmed tortillas, then top with salsa and cabbage slaw.

ALTERNATE COOKING INFORMATION: Chickpeas can also be roasted! Preheat the oven to 400°F and line a baking sheet with foil. Spray with non-stick cooking spray. Toss the chickpeas with the oil, cumin, and salt and bake for 15 to 20 minutes, stirring once halfway through cooking time.

Mushroom and Black Bean Tacos

SERVINGS: 6

I love mushrooms, but my husband isn't a huge fan, and I've figured out a way around that. Instead of slicing the mushrooms or halving them, I chop them up fine. This way they cook down quickly and caramelize. That makes them so yummy and he doesn't even notice them!

For the mushroom and black bean filling:

1 tablespoon extra-virgin olive oil

1 large white onion, chopped

8 ounces mushrooms, cleaned and chopped

¼ teaspoon kosher salt

2 cloves garlic, minced

1½ teaspoons ground cumin

1½ teaspoons chili powder

1 (15-ounce) can black beans, drained and rinsed

2 tablespoons water

2 tablespoons fresh lime juice

For the tacos:

12 (6-inch) corn tortillas, warmed

1 cup lightly packed cilantro leaves

½ small white onion, finely chopped

Toppings: shredded cheddar cheese, plain Greek yogurt or guacamole

To cook the mushrooms and beans:

Set a large skillet over medium heat and add the oil. Once hot, add the onion and cook 5 minutes, stirring frequently. Add mushrooms and cook, stirring until golden, about five minutes. Add the salt and garlic and cook 1 more minute. Add the spices, stirring to toast them and prevent them from burning, another minute more. Stir in the black beans, water, and lime juice and cook 3 to 4 minutes, until most of the liquid has been cooked off.

To make the tacos:

Serve mushroom and black beans in warmed tortillas with cilantro, onions, and any of your other favorite toppings.

GROCERY TIP: Any kind of mushroom will work here, including cremini, mini portobellos, shiitake, button, etc. You can even use a combination of mushrooms for serious umami!

Mediterranean Veggie Tacos

SERVINGS: 4

Raise your hand if you love feta cheese! Now raise it if you love kalamata olives! Ok, I can't see you, but I know you're raising your hand, because I am too! Nothing is better than a bunch of roasted veggies tossed with extra-virgin olive oil, cheese, and olives. Well, the only thing better is turning it into a taco, like I do here!

For the vegetables:

¼ cup extra-virgin olive oil

¼ cup red wine vinegar

½ teaspoon kosher salt

¼ teaspoon freshly ground black pepper

½ teaspoon dried oregano

1 clove garlic, smashed

3 large carrots, peeled and cut into ¼-inch rounds

2 bell peppers (red, orange, yellow or green or combination), large dice

½ medium red onion, peeled and sliced into ½-inch slices

For the tacos:

8 yogurt flatbreads (see page 230) or whole grain pitas, warmed

½ cup plain hummus

¼ cup crumbled feta cheese

½ cup pitted kalamata olives, halved

To prepare the vegetables:

In a gallon-size, sealable plastic bag, combine the oil, vinegar, salt, pepper, oregano, and garlic. Add the vegetables, press out any excess air from the bag, then seal and turn to coat. Marinate for at least 30 minutes and up to 2 hours in the refrigerator.

To cook the vegetables:

Preheat oven to 425°F. Line a large baking sheet with foil and coat with non-stick cooking spray. Using a slotted spoon or spatula, remove vegetables from the marinade and place on the prepared pan, reserving the marinade. Roast for 15 minutes, then add the marinade and toss with the vegetables. Cook for an additional 10 minutes, or until vegetables are lightly brown and crisp tender. Remove from the oven and allow to cool slightly.

To make the tacos:

Portion hummus among flatbreads and top with vegetables. Garnish with feta cheese and kalamata olives.

GROCERY TIP: You can buy flatbreads at the store if you don't have time to make them.

RECIPE NOTE: Want more protein? Add a can of drained chickpeas to the veggie mixture and roast them with the vegetables during the last 10 minutes of cooking.

Turn Up Da Beet Falafel Tacos

SERVINGS 4 TO 8

For the beet falafel:

1 (15-ounce) can beets, drained and rinsed

1 jalapeño pepper, seeded and roughly chopped

3 cloves garlic

1 (15-ounce) can garbanzo beans, drained and rinsed

⅔ cup masa harina

2 tablespoons chopped cilantro

1 tablespoon adobo sauce from canned chipotle chiles in adobo

½ teaspoon kosher salt

For the avocado mash:

1 medium, ripe avocado

1 tablespoon lemon juice

2 tablespoons chopped cilantro

2 tablespoons finely chopped white onion

2 teaspoons finely chopped jalapeño

¼ teaspoon kosher salt

For the tacos:

8 to 16 (6-inch) corn tortillas

½ cup chopped cilantro

2 ounces crumbled cotija cheese

In life, you sometimes get the chance to meet super cool, amazing people. Elizabeth Shaw is one of those people. She is an intelligent and inspiring RD (check her out at ShawSimpleSwaps.com) and fertility advocate (follow her on BumpstoBaby.com). She's my rock, one of my biggest supporters, and she co-authored the Fertility Foods Cookbook *with me. On top of all of that, she's a stellar cook and creator of this super delicious recipe! Love you, Liz!*

To make the beet falafel:

Preheat oven to 375°F and coat a large baking sheet with non-stick cooking spray.

Using a 12-cup food processor add beets, jalapeño pepper, and garlic cloves. Pulse a few times, scrape down the sides of the bowl with a spatula, and pulse a few more times, until chopped. Remove lid, scrape down the sides again, and add in garbanzo beans. Pulse 10 to 12 times, scrape down sides again, process another 20 seconds. Add in masa harina, cilantro, adobo, and salt and process 10 seconds, scrape down, and process another 10 seconds or until combined. Mixture should resemble cookie dough consistency.

Divide batter into 16 equal-sized pieces. Roll each piece into a ball then place on prepared baking sheet. Bake for 25 minutes or until tops are lightly browned.

While falafel is baking, make the avocado mash:

Remove flesh from avocado and add to small bowl. Mash with the back of a fork until smooth. Mix in lemon juice, cilantro, white onion, jalapeño, and salt. Set aside.

. . . continued on next page

To make the tacos:

Warm tortillas and spread avocado mash over the center of each. Add 2 falafels on top and garnish with cotija cheese and chopped cilantro. Enjoy!

SAVING TIP: You'll need to buy a can of chipotles in adobo sauce, which will be more than you need. But here's the good news: these chiles freeze well! Place what you don't need in a small, sealable freezer bag and freeze up to 6 months. Make sure you label the bag so that you know what's in there!

SAVING TIP: Store in an air-tight container in the refrigerator for up to four days or in the freezer for up to three months.

Southwest Black Bean Succo-Tacos

SERVINGS: 4

Succotash is traditionally a mixture of corn and lima beans, but I've given it a southwest twist by swapping in black beans and jalapeño. And it all seems pretty perfect when tucked into a fun little muffin tin taco!

For the tortillas:

12 (6-inch) corn tortillas, room temperature

For the succotash:

2 teaspoons extra-virgin olive oil

1 small yellow onion, chopped

1 red bell pepper, chopped

2 teaspoons chili powder

1 (15-ounce) can black beans, drained and rinsed

1 cup sweet corn (canned or thawed from frozen)

1 tablespoon red wine vinegar

½ teaspoon kosher salt

1 cup shredded sharp cheddar cheese

For the jalapeño yogurt:

¼ cup cilantro, chopped, plus extra for garnish

½ jalapeño, roughly chopped

⅓ cup plain Greek yogurt

1 tablespoon fresh lime juice

⅛ teaspoon kosher salt

To make muffin tin tacos:

Preheat the oven to 350°F. Cut circles out of tortillas using a 4-inch round cookie cutter. Place 1 tortilla round into each cup of a 12-cup muffin tin and press into muffin cups using a juice glass or deep measuring cup. Repeat with remaining tortillas. Set aside.

To make the succotash:

Heat the oil in a large skillet over medium heat. Add the onion and pepper and cook, stirring occasionally, until softened, about 8 minutes. Add the chili powder and cook 1 minute. Stir in the black beans and corn and cook 2 to 3 minutes, until beans and corn are warmed through. Take off the heat and add the red wine vinegar and salt. Portion mixture among the muffin cup tortillas. Top with a sprinkle of cheese and bake 20 minutes.

While tacos are baking, make the jalapeño yogurt:

In a food processor, blend the cilantro, jalapeño, yogurt, lime juice, and salt together until smooth.

To make the tacos:

Add a dollop of jalapeño yogurt to the top of each taco cup and garnish with a little chopped cilantro.

COOKING TIP: If you don't have a 4-inch round cookie cutter, trim off the edges to make a square to help the tortillas fit into the muffin tin. Save the scraps for making the yummy crunchy topping for the West Coast Taco Salad (see page 163).

Grilled Portobello Tacos

SERVINGS: 4

Time to get grilling! Portobellos are perfect for the grill and are perfect for marinades! Those big mushroom caps soak up marinade and hold up well when placed on the grill. This mushroom taco gets even better when topped with a salad made of arugula, fresh lemon juice, and goat cheese!

For the marinade:

¼ cup extra-virgin olive oil

¼ cup balsamic vinegar

4 to 5 sprigs fresh thyme or 2 teaspoons dried thyme

1 clove garlic, smashed

8 ounces (about 3 to 4) Portobello caps, gills removed and washed

1 medium red onion, peeled and cut into ½ inch thick slices

Kosher salt and freshly ground black pepper

For the arugula topping:

1 tablespoon lemon juice

1 tablespoon extra-virgin olive oil

1 teaspoon Dijon mustard

4 cups baby arugula

For the tacos:

8 (6-inch) corn or flour tortillas, warmed

½ cup crumbled goat cheese

For the marinade:

Place the oil, vinegar, thyme, and garlic in a gallon-size, sealable plastic bag. Seal and shake to combine. Add the mushroom caps and the onions and reseal the bag. Carefully massage marinade into vegetables then place in the refrigerator for at least 30 minutes and up to 1 hour.

To cook the vegetables:

Preheat the grill to high heat or set a grill pan over medium-high heat. If using a grill, clean the grill grates and brush them with oil. If using a grill pan, coat pan lightly with oil. Remove vegetables from the marinade. Season lightly with salt and pepper. Place the onion slices on the grill along with the mushroom caps, gill side up, and cook 4 minutes. Flip onions and caps and cook an additional 4 minutes.

To make the arugula topping:

Mix lemon with olive oil and mustard. Add arugula and toss to coat.

To make the tacos:

Slice the grilled Portobello mushrooms and divide among warmed tortillas. Top with arugula mixture and garnish with crumbled goat cheese.

PREP TIP: To remove gills of the mushroom, pull out the stem, then, using a spoon, lightly scrape out the gills and discard. I like to use a grapefruit spoon to do this task!

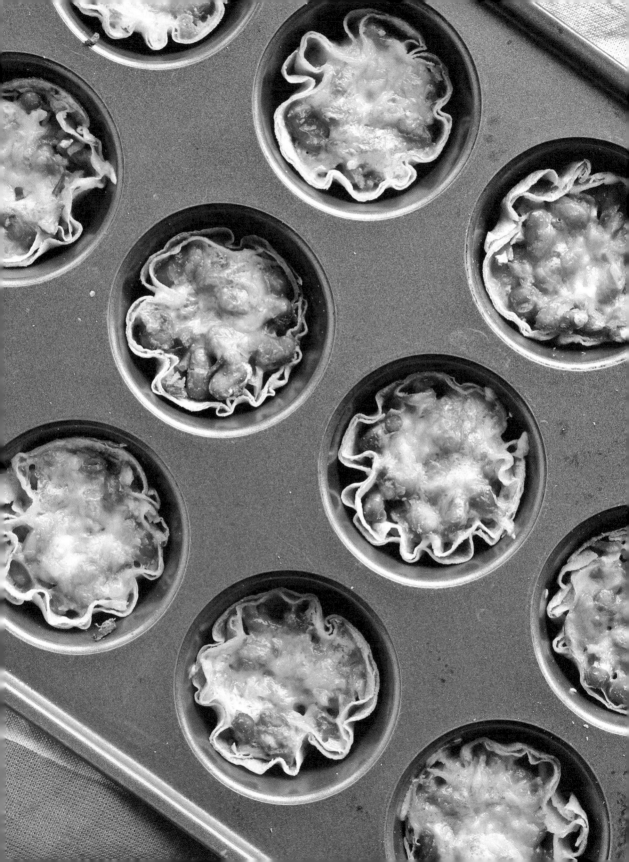

Muffin Tin Bean Tacos

SERVINGS: 8

If you have kids, they'll love helping you make these tacos. Their little hands are perfect for filling those cups with beans and cheese! Easy to make and easy to enjoy!

For the tacos:

24 (6-inch) corn tortillas, warmed

1 (15-ounce) can pinto beans, drained and rinsed

¼ teaspoon kosher salt

1 teaspoon ground cumin

1 cup shredded carrot, chopped

½ small yellow onion, finely chopped

1½ cups shredded cheddar cheese

For the toppings:

Plain Greek yogurt, salsa, seeded or diced avocado

To make the muffin tin tacos:

Preheat the oven to 350°F. Cut circles out of tortillas using a 4-inch round cookie cutter. Place 1 tortilla round into each cup of two, 12-cup muffin tins and press into muffin cups using a juice glass or deep measuring cup. Repeat with remaining tortillas. Set aside.

In a medium bowl, toss beans with salt, cumin, carrot, and onions. Distribute half of the cheese among the tortilla cups. Top with a rounded tablespoon of bean mixture, then remaining cheese. Bake for 20 minutes. Remove from the oven and allow to cool in the pan for 5 minutes.

To serve the tacos:

Carefully remove tacos from the tin then top with yogurt, salsa, and avocado just before serving.

GROCERY TIP: Did you know you can buy pre-shredded carrots? You can, and it's a BIG time saver. I have you chop it here so that it cooks quickly.

COOKING TIP: If you don't have a 4-inch round cookie cutter, trim off the edges to make a square to help the tortillas fit into the muffin tin. Save the scraps for making the yummy crunchy topping for the West Coast Taco Salad (see page 163).

KITCHEN TIP: Did you know that one 15-ounce can of pinto beans is about the equivalent of 1¾ cups of cooked pinto beans? It is, so if you make your beans from scratch, now you've got the substitution information.

SERVING TIP: If you bought bagged, shredded carrots, you could turn them into a salad for the top of these muffin tin tacos. Mix it with a little plain Greek yogurt, ground cumin, a dash of salt, and a squeeze of fresh lime.

Sweet Potato, Lentil, and Kale Tacos

SERVINGS: 4

Ever had lentils in a taco? I didn't think so, but I bet you'll love these. Plus this recipe is EASY! Potatoes get roasted while the lentils cook. Toss the kale into the oven for a few minutes to crisp it up, and then serve it all with a creamy lemon tahini sauce!

For the potatoes and kale:

2 (5-inch) sweet potatoes, skin-on, cut into 1-inch cubes

1 small red onion, diced

¼ teaspoon cayenne pepper

¼ teaspoon freshly ground black pepper

¼ teaspoon + ⅛ teaspoon kosher salt

1 tablespoon + 2 teaspoons extra-virgin olive oil

1 bunch lacinato or dinosaur kale, stemmed and sliced thin

For the lentils:

½ cup dried green or French lentils, picked over and rinsed

1 bay leaf

1 garlic clove, peeled

⅛ teaspoon kosher salt

For the sauce:

1 tablespoon fresh lemon juice

1 tablespoon tahini

1 tablespoon water

For the tacos:

8 hard taco shells or (6-inch) soft corn tortillas, warmed

To cook the vegetables:

Preheat the oven to 400°F. Line a large rimmed baking sheet with foil and coat lightly with nonstick cooking spray. In a medium bowl, combine the sweet potatoes, red onion, cayenne pepper, black pepper, and ¼ teaspoon salt. Add 1 tablespoon of oil and toss to coat.

Spread the potatoes out onto the prepared baking sheet and roast 20 minutes, stirring once after 10 minutes.

To the mixing bowl where the sweet potato was, add the kale and toss with remaining olive oil and salt. Once the sweet potato mixture has cooked for 20 minutes, add the kale to the baking sheet, mix, and cook for an additional 10 minutes.

To cook the lentils:

Place lentils, bay leaf, and garlic in a small pot and add water to cover by about 2 inches. Set pot over medium-high heat and bring to a boil. Reduce heat, partially cover, and simmer for about 20 minutes. Stir in salt and continue to simmer for an additional 5 to 10 minutes, or until lentils are tender. Turn off heat and let sit in pot until ready to serve. Drain just before serving.

To make the sauce:

In a small bowl, whisk together the lemon juice, tahini, and water.

To make the tacos:

Serve lentils in tortillas and top with sweet potato mixture. Drizzle with tahini sauce and enjoy.

Mexican Grilled Corn Tacos

SERVINGS: 4

If you're lucky, you've tried elotes, or grilled ears of corn topped with mayo, chili powder, cheese, and a squeeze of lime juice. Delicious, right? Well, you know I had to make a taco out of that, so welcome to my taco version of elotes.

4 ears sweet corn, husks and silks removed

2 teaspoons vegetable oil

For the sauce and corn:

1 ripe avocado

2 tablespoons extra-virgin olive oil mayonnaise or other mayonnaise

2 tablespoons fresh lime juice

½ teaspoon chili pepper

¼ teaspoon kosher salt

¼ teaspoon freshly ground black pepper

⅓ cup crumbled feta or cojita cheese

½ small red onion, finely chopped

1 cup cilantro, roughly chopped

For the tacos:

½ cup toasted pepitas (pumpkin seeds)

½ cup radishes, thinly sliced

1 cup tomatoes, chopped

8 hard taco shells, warmed

To cook the corn:

Preheat the grill to medium-high heat or set a grill pan over medium-high heat. Brush the corn with oil and grill, turning corn often, to cook and char, about 10 minutes. Remove from the grill or grill pan and set on a plate to cool. Once cooled, cut the corn from the cob (see tip) and place in a medium bowl.

To make the sauce and corn:

Mash ½ of the avocado in a small bowl and then add the mayo, lime juice, chili pepper, salt, and pepper.

Add the sauce to the bowl with the corn, along with the cheese, red onion, and cilantro. Toss to combine.

To make the tacos:

Serve corn mixture in warmed taco shells and top with pepitas, radishes, and tomatoes. Slice the remaining avocado and use as garnish, along with any leftover cilantro.

PREP TIP: Remove the corn from the cob by holding the cob upright inside a shallow bowl. The smaller end should be facing the ceiling and the larger end should be resting on the bottom of the bowl. Using a sharp knife, cut downwards on the cob to remove the kernels. Continue around the cob until all of the corn is off.

ALTERNATE COOKING INFORMATION: Set a heavy non-stick pan, such as cast iron, over medium-high heat. Add the oil. Once hot, add 3 cups drained, canned corn (pat corn dry for best results) and cook, stirring occasionally, until corn is charred, about 10 minutes. Proceed with recipe as above.

RECIPE NOTE: Looking for additional protein? You could easily add a can of garbanzo or pinto beans or even cooked shredded chicken to this dish.

COOKING TIP: To toast the pepitas, place them in a skillet set over medium heat. Cook the pepitas, shaking the pan occasionally to prevent them from burning, about 3 to 4 minutes.

Sesame Bok Choy Tacos

SERVINGS: 4

I was introduced to bok choy in culinary school and I could not get over how much I loved it! It's one of those vegetables that just makes me happy, and I love this recipe because it's loaded with plenty of it. Enjoy it in a savory crepe or flour tortilla, or even a big lettuce leaf taco!

For the sauce:

2 cloves garlic, minced

2 tablespoons white miso

2 tablespoons low-sodium soy sauce

⅛ to ¼ teaspoon crushed red pepper

For the vegetables:

1 tablespoon vegetable oil

½ pound bok choy, trimmed and sliced thin

1 red bell pepper, thinly sliced

2 cups snow peas, trimmed

1 cup shelled, frozen edamame, thawed

1 teaspoon sesame oil

1 teaspoon rice vinegar

For the tacos:

8 savory crepes (see page 217) or (6-inch) flour tortillas, warmed

2 teaspoons white or black sesame seeds

To make the sauce:

Mix garlic, miso, soy sauce and crushed red pepper in a bowl.

To cook the vegetables:

Heat oil in a wok or large, deep-sided non-stick skillet over medium-high heat. Once hot, add the bok choy, bell pepper, and snow peas and cook 3 minutes, stirring occasionally. Add the edamame and cook 2 more minutes. Add the sauce to the skillet and cook 1 minute. Remove from heat and stir in the sesame oil and rice vinegar.

To make the tacos:

Serve vegetables in crepes or tortillas then garnish with sesame seeds.

RECIPE NOTE: Looking for some additional protein? Why not toss in some sautéed or baked cubed tofu!

Cauliflower Rice Tacos

SERVINGS: 4

Sometimes it's hard to eat enough vegetables each day. I get it! That's why I love these Cauliflower Rice Tacos. Ricing cauliflower makes it the perfect size for taco filling, and when you add traditional taco flavors, you won't even believe you're eating cauliflower.

For the cauliflower rice:

1 head cauliflower

2 tablespoons extra-virgin olive oil + extra for coating pan

⅛ teaspoon kosher salt

1 tablespoon + 1 teaspoon taco salt-free taco seasoning

For the tacos:

8 (6-inch) corn tortillas or hard taco shells, warmed

4 cups shredded lettuce

1 small jalapeño, sliced

¼ cup toasted pepitas

3 large carrots. shredded (or about 2 cups shredded)

½ cup salsa of your choice or pico de gallo

1 cup Super Simple Homemade Guacamole (see page 229)

To prepare the cauliflower rice:

Core and peel away leaves of cauliflower. Break into pieces and rinse under cold water. Run through a salad spinner or pat dry with a clean towel.

Working in ½ cup batches, add the cauliflower to a food processor, and pulse until cauliflower resembles rice. Remove and repeat with remaining cauliflower.

To make the tacos:

Preheat the oven to 425°F and coat a large baking sheet lightly with olive oil.

To a large bowl, add the riced cauliflower, olive oil, salt, and taco seasoning. Mix well until combined and spread evenly on the prepared baking sheet. Bake for 20 minutes, stirring halfway through cooking time. For crispier cauliflower, cook a little longer, stirring every 5 minutes until desired doneness.

Serve cauliflower in warmed tortillas then top with shredded lettuce, jalapeño, pepitas, carrots, salsa, and guacamole.

GROCERY TIP: You can actually buy cauliflower rice at the grocery store! Save time by buying the pre-riced version.

SERVING TIP: Want more "oomph" in these tacos? Try adding warmed black or pinto beans to the tacos, too.

Roasted Chickpea Tabbouleh Tacos

SERVINGS: 4 TO 6

For the chickpeas:

1 (15.5-ounce) can chickpeas, drained and rinsed

1 tablespoon extra-virgin olive oil

¼ teaspoon kosher salt

¼ teaspoon freshly ground black pepper

For the tahini dressing:

1 tablespoon tahini

1 lemon, zest and juice

2 tablespoons extra-virgin olive oil

¼ teaspoon kosher salt

⅛ teaspoon freshly ground black pepper

For the tabbouleh:

1 small red onion, chopped

1 red bell pepper, chopped

½ cucumber, seeded and chopped

1 cup lightly packed fresh mint, chopped

1 cup lightly packed parsley, chopped

For the tacos:

8 hard taco shells, warmed

½ cup crumbled feta cheese

Chickpeas again! And this time, they're roasted! If you haven't roasted chickpeas before, then now is the time. That crunchy goodness should not be missed! Those crispy bites taste great too when they're tossed with a tahini dressing and served in a warm taco shell.

To cook the beans:

Preheat the oven to 400°F and line a medium baking sheet with foil. Toss the chickpeas with the olive oil, salt, and black pepper then spread out onto the baking sheet. Roast for 20 minutes, stirring halfway through cooking time.

While the beans are roasting, make the dressing:

To a small bowl add the tahini and lemon zest and juice. Whisk until combined, then whisk in the olive oil, salt, and pepper. Reserve.

To make the tabbouleh:

Remove beans from the oven and allow them to cool slightly. Add cooled beans to a large bowl along with the onion, pepper, cucumber, mint, and parsley. Add the dressing and toss to combine.

To make the tacos:

Portion tabbouleh among warmed taco shells and garnish with feta cheese.

GROCERY TIP: Looking for tahini at your grocery store? It can sometimes be found in the section with nut butters, but if it's not there, look for it in the ethnic aisle.

PREP TIP: Save time by cutting veggies just after you make the dressing and while those beans are still cooking!

RECIPE NOTE: Too much herb for you? That's okay! Feel free to adjust the parsley and mint to reflect your preferences.

Vegetarian Sloppy Joe Tacos

SERVINGS: 4

Is there anything better than a sloppy Joe? Something about all of that sauce getting soaked up by a hamburger bun—yum! My vegetarian version elicits those same flavors, but without the meat and no bun! It's delicious, and hopefully not too sloppy!

For the sloppy Joes:

1 tablespoon extra-virgin olive oil

4 ounces mushrooms, cleaned and finely chopped

½ medium white onion, finely chopped

1 red bell pepper, chopped

2 teaspoons chili powder

1 teaspoon ground cumin

2 tablespoons tomato paste

1 (14.5-ounce) can no-salt-added crushed tomatoes

2 teaspoons packed light brown sugar

2 teaspoons molasses

1 (15-ounce) can no-salt-added pinto or black beans, drained and rinsed

Kosher salt

For the tacos:

8 hard taco shells, warmed

Optional toppings: diced white onion, chopped dill pickles

To make the sloppy Joes:

Set a large skillet over medium-high heat and add the oil. Once hot, add the mushrooms and cook 3 minutes. Add a pinch of salt and cook 5 more minutes. Add the onion and bell pepper to the skillet and cook, stirring often, about 5 to 6 minutes, until vegetables are softened. Add the chili powder and cumin and cook 1 minute, stirring frequently. Mix in the tomato paste, tomatoes and their juices, brown sugar, and molasses. Add the black beans, then bring to a simmer and cook, partially covered, about 30 minutes and up to 1 hour. Season to taste with salt. (If sloppy Joe mixture hasn't thickened, remove lid and turn up the heat to cook off some of the liquid.)

To make the tacos:

Serve sloppy Joe in warmed shells with onion and chopped pickles, if desired.

PREP TIP: Save time by chopping the onion and mushrooms in a food processor!

COOKING TIP: Cooking this dish longer helps develop flavor. But if you're strapped for time, 20 to 30 minutes is just long enough to get the job done, too.

TACO SALAD RECIPES

No taco cookbook is complete without a few good taco salad recipes, right? Expect some pretty non-traditional taco salads in this section! I've got everything from crab cakes to ginger-miso dressing! Because in my mind, taco salads are more fun when made with an unexpected twist!

Tex Mex Taco Salad

SERVINGS: 4

For the beef:

2 teaspoons extra-virgin olive oil

½ medium onion, diced

1 pound 90% lean ground beef

1 teaspoon ground cumin

1 to 2 tablespoons chili powder

1 (14.5-ounce) can crushed tomatoes

For the dressing:

½ cup plain Greek yogurt

2 tablespoons fresh lime juice

½ teaspoon ground cumin

¼ teaspoon garlic powder

1 tablespoon water

½ teaspoon honey

⅛ teaspoon kosher salt

For the salad:

8 cups chopped lettuce, such as romaine or other lettuce of your choice

4 cups tortilla chips, lightly crushed

Optional fixings: chopped tomatoes, sliced jalapeño, shredded cheese, pinto or black beans

When I was little, we occasionally went to chain Mexican restaurants. I was always fascinated by that ginormous tortilla bowl filled with taco meat and lettuce. I had it once and I wasn't impressed. But now, I see it has promise, so that's why I made this version! Loaded with ground beef simmered in tomatoes and spices, plenty of lettuce, and a tangy Greek yogurt dressing that won't leave you feeling heavy, just satisfied.

To cook the beef:

Heat the oil in a large skillet set over medium heat. Once hot, add the onion and cook, stirring occasionally, until softened, about 8 to 10 minutes. Increase the heat to medium-high, then add the beef and cook, stirring to crumble, until browned, about 5 minutes. Drain fat, then add cumin and chili powder and cook 1 minute. Add canned tomatoes and scrape the bottom of the pan to remove any browned bits. Reduce heat to medium low, partially cover, and simmer 10 minutes and up to 30 minutes.

To make the dressing:

Combine the Greek yogurt, lime juice, cumin, garlic powder, water, honey and salt in a small bowl and mix until well-incorporated.

To make the taco salad:

Portion lettuce among plates. Top with beef mixture, the dressing, crushed tortilla chips, and your favorite fixings.

West Coast Taco Salad

SERVINGS: 4

Okay, I love this recipe so much! This is the kind of salad that makes me happy. Tons of flavor, loads of veggies, some good lean protein, and a dressing that's fresh and fun. It's truly a bowl of happiness. Does that mean I should move to the West Coast? I think so!

For the marinade/dressing:

2 tablespoons white miso

2 teaspoons minced fresh ginger

2 tablespoons rice wine vinegar

2 tablespoons fresh lime juice

½ cup vegetable oil

1 pound boneless, skinless chicken breasts, pounded to ½ inch thickness

For tortilla strips:

4 (6-inch) corn tortillas, thinly sliced

1 tablespoon extra-virgin olive oil

½ teaspoon kosher salt

For the salad:

8 cups chopped lettuce, such as romaine

2 green onions, white and light green parts only, thinly sliced

1 cup alfalfa or other sprouts

1 ripe avocado, seeded and sliced

1 pint cherry tomatoes

1 tablespoon toasted sesame seeds

To make the marinade/dressing:

Whisk together the miso, ginger, rice wine vinegar, lime juice, and oil. Remove and reserve a ¼ cup of the marinade. Transfer the remaining marinade to a gallon-size, sealable bag. Add the chicken, press out any excess air from the bag, then seal and turn to coat. Marinate for at least 30 minutes and up to 1 hour in the refrigerator.

To make the tortilla strips:

Preheat the oven to 375°F. Toss the tortilla strips with the oil and salt. Spread strips out in a single layer onto a large parchment-lined baking pan. Bake 10 minutes, give a stir, then bake an additional 5 to 8 minutes, or until crispy.

To cook the chicken:

Preheat the grill to medium-high heat or set a grill pan over medium-high heat. If using a grill, clean the grill grates and brush them with oil. If using a grill pan, coat pan lightly with oil. Remove chicken from the marinade, pat dry; discard marinade. Grill chicken about 8 minutes on each side, until internal temperature reaches 165°F. Let rest 5 minutes before slicing.

To make the taco salad:

Slice the chicken. Portion lettuce in the bottom of a large serving bowl. Top with sliced chicken, green onions,

. . . continued on next page

sprouts, avocado, tomatoes, and sesame seeds. Add dressing and toss to combine. Garnish salad with tortilla strips just before serving.

ALTERNATE COOKING INFORMATION: Don't feel like grilling? No problem! You can bake the chicken, too! Preheat the oven to 375°F. Remove chicken from the marinade and pat dry; discard marinade. Place on a rimmed baking sheet coated with non-stick cooking spray. Cook 15 to 18 minutes, until internal temperature reaches 165°F.

COOKING TIP: Make sure you use a large baking sheet to cook those tortilla strips. The more room you have, the crispier they can get. And if 15 to 18 minutes doesn't seem long enough, keep them in the oven for a few additional minutes. Let them cool completely on a rack before adding them to the salad.

East Coast Taco Salad

For the crab cakes:

2 teaspoons Dijon mustard

3 tablespoons plain Greek yogurt

2 tablespoons finely chopped parsley

½ teaspoon kosher salt

¼ teaspoon freshly ground black pepper

1 large egg, beaten

⅓ cup finely crushed tortilla chips

12 ounces lump crab meat, picked over to remove any shell pieces

All-purpose flour, for dusting

2 tablespoons vegetable oil

For the dressing:

¼ cup plain Greek yogurt

2 tablespoons mayonnaise

1 teaspoon Old Bay seasoning

1 tablespoon lemon juice

1 teaspoon lemon zest

For serving:

8 cups romaine lettuce, chopped

3 large carrots, shredded (about 2 cups shredded)

1 to 2 ripe tomatoes, chopped

1 to 2 cups tortilla chips, lightly crushed

Channeling my inner Bostonian, I decided to take a swing at making crab cakes. And I love the result! Using crunchy tortilla chips as a binder works so well here, and I like serving this one topped with crunchy corn tortilla chips, but you can also serve this salad in mini taco shell bowls (see Midwest Taco Salad, see page 166 for instructions on how to make taco bowls).

To make the crab cakes:

In a medium bowl, whisk together the mustard, yogurt, parsley, salt, pepper, and egg. Add the crushed tortilla chips and the crabmeat and using clean hands, gently toss together.

Using a ¼-cup measuring cup, scoop out crab mixture and then shape into patties. Place on a parchment lined baking sheet and stick in the freezer for 30 minutes.

To cook the crab cakes:

Dust crab cakes lightly with flour. Heat half of the oil in a large, heavy pan, such as cast iron. Add half of the crab cakes and cook over medium-high heat, about 4 to 5 minutes per side. Keep warm as you cook remaining crab cakes. Repeat the process with the remaining oil and crab cakes.

To make the dressing:

Place the yogurt, mayonnaise, Old Bay seasoning, lemon juice, and zest in a bowl, whisk until combined.

To make the taco salad:

Toss the romaine with the carrot and place on plates. Top with tomatoes, crushed tortilla chips, and 2 crab cakes. Drizzle with dressing and serve with lemon wedge.

RECIPE NOTE: Use any flour here for dusting. Even gluten-free flours work!

Midwest (Chicken Salad) Taco Salad

SERVINGS: 4 TO 6

Like tuna salad, chicken salad has been a staple in my life since I was little. My mom used to make a version that was simply chicken, black olives, a little onion, and some mayo. That's it. Simple ingredients, but it was always so delicious. I mimic that recipe here, and, of course, add a few more ingredients and serve it all in tortilla bowls!

For the chicken salad:

3 tablespoons extra-virgin olive oil mayonnaise

2 tablespoons plain Greek yogurt

1 tablespoon fresh lemon juice

Pinch cayenne pepper

¼ teaspoon kosher salt

¼ teaspoon freshly ground black pepper

½ small white onion, finely diced

1 large celery stalk, finely chopped

3 cups cooked chicken, cubed

1 (2.25-ounce) can sliced black olives, drained

For the tacos:

4 cups lettuce, chopped

1 medium tomato, chopped

1 cup sweet corn

For the taco bowls:

4 (6-inch) flour tortillas

To make the chicken salad:

In a large mixing bowl, whisk together the mayonnaise, Greek yogurt, lemon juice, cayenne, salt, and pepper. Stir in the onion and celery, then add the chicken and olives and toss to combine. Cover and refrigerate for at least 1 hour.

To make the tortilla bowls:

Preheat oven to 375°F. Flip a 12 cup muffin tin over. Nestle 4 of the tortillas between the cups, forming bowls. Place on the middle rack in the oven and cook for about 15 minutes. Let cool in pan slightly. Repeat with remaining tortillas.

To make the taco salad:

Portion lettuce inside cooled tortilla bowls. Top with chicken salad, tomatoes, and corn and enjoy.

RECIPE NOTE: See recipe for Easy Poached Chicken (see page 49) to use for "cooked chicken" in this recipe. Or simply purchase a rotisserie chicken from the grocery store to make things faster.

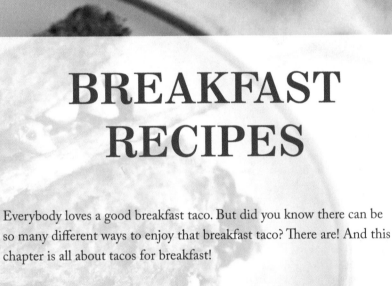

BREAKFAST RECIPES

Everybody loves a good breakfast taco. But did you know there can be so many different ways to enjoy that breakfast taco? There are! And this chapter is all about tacos for breakfast!

Fried Egg Tacos with Dukka

SERVINGS: 4

For the dukka:

¼ cup raw hazelnuts

¼ cup whole, raw almonds

¼ cup shelled, raw pistachios

1 tablespoon sesame seeds

1 tablespoon coriander seeds

2 teaspoons cumin seeds

Kosher salt and freshly cracked pepper

For the salad:

1 tablespoon tahini

1 tablespoon lemon juice

2 tablespoons water

1 tablespoon plain Greek yogurt

1 small clove garlic, finely minced

1 teaspoon lemon zest

4 cups baby arugula

Kosher salt and freshly ground black pepper

For the tacos:

2 tablespoons + 2 teaspoons olive or vegetable oil

8 large eggs

Kosher salt

8 (6-inch) corn or flour tortillas, warmed

Here's the truth: I used to be scared of a runny yolk. There was just something so "wrong" about that yellow yolk running all over my plate. But now, I know everything about that runny yolk is so "right." And I really enjoy pairing fried eggs with everything. This homemade dukka, a blend of nuts and seeds used in Egyptian cooking, is so incredibly interesting and flavorful and pairs so well with that creamy, runny egg!

To make the dukka:

Set a medium non-stick skillet over medium heat. Add the hazelnuts, almonds, and pistachios. Cook, shaking pan occasionally, until nuts are toasted and fragrant, about 2 to 3 minutes. Once cool, coarsely chop and transfer to a medium bowl.

In the same skillet, toast the sesame seeds in the same way, cooking about 1 minute. Transfer to the bowl with the nuts.

To the same skillet, add the coriander and cumin seeds and cook, shaking the pan often, until fragrant, about 1 minute. Transfer coriander and cumin to a mortar and pestle or spice grinder. Once cool, crush or process. Add to the bowl. Toss everything together.

To make the salad:

In a small bowl, whisk together the tahini, lemon juice, water, yogurt, garlic and lemon zest. Season to taste with salt and black pepper. Add the arugula then toss to combine just before serving.

To fry the eggs:

Set the non-stick skillet back over medium heat, add 1 to 2 teaspoons oil, and, once hot, add 1 or 2 cracked eggs. Season with salt to taste. Cook 2 minutes, cover

. . . continued on next page

with foil, and cook an additional 2 to 3 minutes, or until desired doneness. Repeat with remaining eggs.

To make the tacos:

Serve dressed salad in warmed tortillas topped with fried eggs and dukka.

KITCHEN TIP: No mortar and pestle and no spice grinder? No problem! Place seeds in a sturdy plastic bag, such as a freezer bag. Using a rolling pin or meat mallet or pan, crush the seeds.

SAVING TIP: Save extra dukka to use as a topping for salad, toast, or fish or mix it into hummus. Store it in an air-tight container in the fridge and use within 1 week.

Everyday Breakfast Tacos

SERVINGS: 4

Is life possible without a good breakfast taco? I think not! Is there really anything better than scrambled eggs wrapped in tortillas along with beans and cheese? Top it with guacamole and plain Greek yogurt and I'm in heaven.

For the eggs:

8 large eggs

¼ cup milk

½ teaspoon kosher salt

¼ teaspoon freshly ground black pepper

For the tacos:

4 (6-inch) corn or flour tortillas, warmed

1 cup shredded cheddar cheese

1 (15-ounce) can black beans, drained, rinsed and warmed

Toppings: Salsa, plain Greek yogurt, diced avocado

Optional extras:

Cooked veggies such as onion, bell peppers, or mushrooms

Chopped raw spinach or sprouts

Pickled veggies

Chopped bacon

To cook the eggs:

In a bowl, whisk the eggs with the milk, then pour into a large non-stick pan and cook for one minute. Do not stir. Using a spatula, gently fold and lift the egg mixture, allowing the uncooked portions to flow under and cook. Cook for 3 to 4 minutes, or until eggs are cooked but still moist. If adding any "extras," stir them in during the last few minutes of cooking.

To make the tacos:

Serve eggs on warmed tortillas with cheese, beans, salsa, yogurt and avocado.

COOKING TIP: Want to jazz up those beans? Heat 1 teaspoon oil in a small pot over medium heat. Add 1 teaspoon ground cumin and 2 teaspoons chili powder. Cook 1 minute, then add drained beans; toss to coat.

Baleada Tacos

SERVINGS: 4

For the beans:

1 tablespoon vegetable oil

½ medium white onion, minced

1 garlic clove, finely chopped

½ teaspoon ground cumin

1 (15.5-ounce) can kidney or pinto beans, drained and rinsed

2 tablespoons plain Greek yogurt

2 tablespoons + 1 teaspoon fresh lime or lemon juice

For the eggs:

6 large eggs

¼ cup milk

For the tacos:

¼ cup cotija or feta cheese

¼ cup plain Greek yogurt

1 ripe avocado, seeded and sliced

¼ cup sliced canned or jarred pickled jalapeños, if desired

1 to 2 cups shredded green or purple cabbage, if desired

4 (6-inch) flour tortillas

A baleada is a traditional Honduran dish made with eggs, kidney beans, and cheese all rolled up in a tortilla. Of course, there are many variations, and mine stays pretty true to the classic dish, but feel free to experiment with different beans or toppings to make the dish your own!

To cook the beans:

Heat the oil in a large non-stick skillet set over medium heat. Add the onion and cook 5 minutes, stirring often. Add the garlic and cumin and cook 1 more minute. Stir in the kidney beans and cook 1 to 2 more minutes. Then stir in Greek yogurt and lime juice. Season to taste with salt and black pepper. Remove from heat and mash to desired consistency with a fork or potato masher. (If your mashed beans are on the thick side, add a little bit of water to thin to desired consistency.)

To scramble the eggs:

In a bowl, whisk the eggs with the milk, then pour into a large non-stick pan and cook for one minute. Do not stir. Using a spatula, gently fold and lift the egg mixture, allowing the uncooked portions to flow under and cook. Cook for 3 to 4 minutes, or until eggs are cooked but still moist.

To make the tacos:

Spread beans evenly among tortillas and top with scrambled eggs. Garnish with cheese, yogurt, avocado, pickled jalapeños, and cabbage.

PREP TIP: In a rush? Go ahead and buy a can of refried beans. Already have cooked beans on hand? Lucky you! Replace the 15-ounce can with 1 ¾ cup cooked beans.

RECIPE NOTE: Don't want to use vegetable oil? That's cool. You can replace it in many of these recipes with other high-smoke point oils, such as grapeseed or canola oil.

Baharat Bean Tacos with Fried Eggs

SERVINGS: 4

For the Baharat beans:

⅛ teaspoon ground allspice

¼ teaspoon freshly ground black pepper

⅛ teaspoon ground cardamom

¼ teaspoon ground cloves

½ teaspoon ground coriander seed

¼ teaspoon ground cinnamon

¼ teaspoon ground cumin

⅛ teaspoon ground nutmeg

1 tablespoon water

1 tablespoon extra-virgin olive oil

1 (15-ounce) can garbanzo beans, drained and rinsed

¼ teaspoon kosher salt

For the eggs:

2 teaspoons extra-virgin olive oil

4 large eggs

For the topping:

4 cups mixed baby lettuce

1 tablespoon fresh lemon juice

1 teaspoon fresh lemon zest

For the tacos:

4 (6-inch) corn tortillas, warmed

What is Baharat, you ask? It's a blend of spices used in Middle Eastern cooking. And when they're toasted in a pan with a little oil, they make your whole house smell amazing. I use them here to season beans, which get placed on tortillas and then topped with a fried egg.

To make the Baharat beans:

Mix the spices and water together in a medium mixing bowl. Set aside.

Heat the oil in a medium non-stick sauté pan over medium heat. Once the oil is hot, add the spices mixture and cook, stirring constantly, until fragrant, about 1 minute. Add the drained beans and salt and cook, an additional 2 to 3 minutes, or until beans are warmed through. Transfer mixture back to the medium bowl, and mash with a fork. Cover and keep warm while cooking the eggs.

To cook the eggs:

Set the non-stick skillet back over medium heat and add 1 teaspoon oil. Once hot, add 2 cracked eggs; season with salt and pepper. Cook 2 minutes, cover with foil, and cook an additional 2 to 3 minutes or until desired doneness. Repeat with remaining eggs.

While eggs are cooking, toss the lettuce with the remaining lemon juice and zest.

To make the tacos:

Spread ¼ cup of the bean mixture on each tortilla. Top with a fried egg and the dressed greens.

RECIPE NOTE: There are quite a few spices used here, but I promise the blend is worth the effort. If you have a store that allows you to buy in bulk, do just that. That way you only have to buy a little bit of each of them.

SAVING TIP: Extra Baharat can be refrigerated for a few weeks. Place in a container with a lid and keep refrigerated until needed. Baharat tastes great on top of chicken, hummus, and plenty of other dishes, too!

Feta Bruschetta Frittata Tacos

SERVINGS: 4

Frittatas make for pretty tasty breakfast food. Okay, a pretty tasty anytime food! This one gets topped with a bruschetta made from fresh ripe tomatoes, basil, and red onion and finished with a simple balsamic reduction.

For the bruschetta:

1½ cups fresh tomato, seeded and diced

1 cup fresh basil, thinly sliced

1 tablespoon red onion, finely chopped

1 clove garlic, minced

For the balsamic reduction:

½ cup balsamic vinegar

For the frittata:

6 large eggs

¼ cup milk

½ teaspoon kosher salt

¼ teaspoon freshly ground black pepper

2 teaspoons extra-virgin olive oil

½ cup crumbled feta cheese

For the tacos:

8 hard taco shells, warmed

To make the bruschetta topping:

In a medium bowl, combine the tomato, basil, onion, and garlic. Add a pinch of salt and black pepper and toss to combine.

To make balsamic reduction:

Set a small sauce pot over medium-high heat and add the balsamic vinegar. Simmer the vinegar until reduced by half, about 15 minutes. (You may need to reduce the heat towards the end of cooking.)

To make the frittata:

Position oven rack 5 to 6 inches from the heating element and preheat the broiler. In a large bowl, whisk together the eggs, milk, salt, and pepper. Heat the oil in a 10-inch ovenproof non-stick skillet over medium heat. Pour the eggs into the pan and cook over medium-low heat until the eggs are just set around the edges, about 5 minutes. Sprinkle the top with feta cheese and place the pan in the oven. Broil for about 5 minutes, or until eggs are completely set. Remove from the oven and allow to cool 5 minutes before slicing.

To make the tacos:

Cut frittata into 8 wedges and place into warmed taco shells. Top with bruschetta mixture and garnish with balsamic reduction.

RECIPE NOTE: No time to make the balsamic reduction? Don't sweat it! Just swap in a drizzle of regular balsamic vinegar. But trust me, you should make the reduction—it's DELICIOUS!

Hard Boiled Egg Tacos with Crispy Bacon and Spicy Avocado Cream

SERVINGS: 4

Eggs and bacon are a perfect combination. I love them paired with this spicy avocado cream sauce, too! This meal is perfect for a lazy Sunday breakfast.

For the eggs and bacon:

8 large eggs

8 bacon slices

For the spicy avocado cream salad:

½ ripe avocado

2 tablespoons plain Greek yogurt

1 teaspoon tabasco sauce or other hot sauce

1 tablespoon fresh lime juice

1 heart romaine lettuce, thinly sliced

For the tacos:

Kosher salt and freshly ground black pepper

8 (6-inch) flour tortillas, warmed

2 tablespoons chopped, fresh chives

To cook the eggs:

Place the eggs in the bottom of a large pot, big enough so that the eggs have a little space around them. Add enough water to cover them by 1 inch. Set the pot over medium-high heat and bring to a boil. Once boiling, remove from heat and cover with a lid. Let sit in the pot for 12 minutes, then drain and run under cold water to cool. Once cool, peel the eggs, discarding the shell.

To cook the bacon:

Set a large, non-stick skillet over medium heat. Add half of the bacon and cook, turning frequently, until crisp, about 8 to 10 minutes. Using tongs, transfer bacon to a paper towel-lined plate. Cover with another paper towel and pat dry. Repeat the process with the remaining bacon.

To make the spicy avocado cream:

In a food processor, combine the avocado flesh, yogurt, tabasco sauce, and lime juice. Blend until smooth. Transfer to a medium bowl and add the lettuce. Toss to combine.

To make the tacos:

Slice the eggs and sprinkle with salt and black pepper. Divide them and the bacon slices among the tortillas and top with a sprinkling of chives. Garnish with spicy avocado cream salad.

PB and Macerated Berry Jam Tacos

SERVINGS: 4

I adore peanut butter and I eat it nearly every day (I know, it's kind of a problem). It's such a perfect food, and I really like pairing it with my homemade jam. This recipe allows you to customize your jam, too! Pick your favorite berries or a combination of your favorites!

For the jam:

5 ounces frozen, unsweetened berries of your choice

1 tablespoon granulated sugar

2 teaspoons water

For the tacos:

4 to 6 whole grain bread slices, crusts removed

1 to 2 teaspoons butter

2 tablespoons natural peanut butter

4 tablespoons salted peanuts, chopped

For the jam:

Add the berries, sugar, and water to a small sauce pot and stir. Set pot over medium-high heat and bring to a boil. Reduce heat and simmer, cooking and smashing the fruit with the back of a spoon occasionally, until jammy consistency, about 18 to 20 minutes.

For the tacos:

Roll out the bread slices until thin and pliable. Set a medium non-stick skillet over medium heat. Add butter. Once melted, swirl around the pan, add a few bread slices, and cook 1 minute. Flip and cook the other side. Remove from heat and repeat with the remaining bread slices.

To make the tacos:

Spread peanut butter over the middle portion of each bread slice. Portion 2 tablespoons of the jam on top of the peanut butter, then top with chopped peanuts.

RECIPE NOTE: If you love peanut butter, feel free to add a little more than what's listed here.

COOKING TIP: If you're using a tart berry or a berry that isn't quite ripe, you may need to add a little additional sugar. Add by the ½ teaspoon until it tastes sweet enough.

Cinnamon French Toast Taco

SERVINGS: 4

Of course, I had to make a French Toast Taco! It just makes sense, right? And French Toast makes the perfect holder for your favorite breakfast foods—eggs, bacon, and sausage!

For the French toast:

3 large eggs

2 tablespoons confectioner's sugar

1 cup milk

½ teaspoon pure vanilla extract

¼ teaspoon ground cinnamon

8 slices whole wheat bread

For the eggs:

4 large eggs

2 tablespoons milk

For the tacos:

4 turkey bacon slices or sausage patties, cooked

To make the French toast:

In a large bowl, whisk together the eggs and the confectioner's sugar. Stream in the milk, then add the vanilla and cinnamon.

Set a large non-stick skillet over medium heat. Spray with nonstick cooking spray or melt a little butter in the pan. Dip slices of bread in egg batter, ensuring they're evenly coated. Hold them over the bowl to let excess batter drip off before adding to the hot skillet. Cook about 3 to 4 minutes on each side. Repeat the process for remaining bread slices. Hold toast in a warm (300°F) oven until ready to serve.

To cook the eggs:

In a bowl, whisk the eggs with the milk and season with salt and pepper. Pour the egg mixture into a large non-stick pan and cook for one minute. Do not stir. Using a spatula, gently fold and lift the egg mixture, allowing the uncooked portions to flow under and cook. Cook for 3 to 4 minutes, or until eggs are cooked but still moist.

To make the tacos:

Top each toast slice with eggs and bacon or sausage, fold up like a taco, and enjoy.

PREP TIP: Drier, stale bread works best here. To achieve that, leave bread out, open to the air overnight.

COOKING TIP: You may notice the confectioner's sugar is a bit lumpy when you add it to the eggs. You can prevent this by sifting the sugar into the bowl first, or by simply whisking until the lumps go away.

SERVING TIP: You can also fill this "taco" with fresh fruit and a little plain yogurt!

DESSERT RECIPES

Yes, you can have dessert, too! And guess what?! Most of these taco desserts are little—or perhaps I should say just the right size. These tacos are not only delicious, but perfectly portioned to satisfy any sweet tooth, especially yours!

Fruit Pizza Tacos

SERVINGS: 10

Am I the only one who's eaten countless fruit pizzas? When I was younger, I think everyone served these at every party or occasion. I wasn't upset by that, either, because I loved fruit pizza. And of course you can turn a fruit pizza into a taco! Just use a sugar cookie base and you're good to go!

For the dough:

½ teaspoon baking powder

½ cup white whole wheat flour

¾ cup all-purpose flour

¼ teaspoon kosher salt

¼ cup + 1 tablespoon butter, softened

⅓ cup granulated sugar

1 large egg

1 teaspoon pure vanilla extract

For the cream cheese filling:

2 ounces Neufchâtel cheese

½ teaspoon vanilla extract

1 cup confectioners' sugar

For the top:

Blueberries, sliced kiwi, sliced strawberries or any of your favorite fruits

Get started:

Preheat the oven to 375°F and line two large baking sheets with parchment paper. In a medium bowl, combine the baking powder, flours, and salt. Set aside.

Beat the butter in a large mixing bowl or in the bowl of a stand mixer until fluffy. Add the sugar and beat until sugar is well incorporated, about 2 minutes.

Add the egg and the vanilla extract and beat for two more minutes. Then, gradually add the dry mixture and beat until combined.

While cookies are baking, make the foil rods for draping:

Take two big pieces of foil and shape into 1½ inch logs. You'll be using these to drape the cookies over after they're cooked. This will help shape them into tacos.

To bake the cookies:

Shape into 20 equal-sized balls and place on prepared pans. Smash each gently with a clean hand until slightly flattened, and bake 8 minutes. Allow to cool slightly before draping over the foil rod. (It's ok if they crack!)

While cookies are baking, make the cream cheese filling:

In a large mixing bowl, whisk the cheese with the vanilla extract. Gradually add confectioner's sugar and mix until smooth and creamy.

To serve:

Spread some of the cream cheese filling on each sugar cookie "taco," then top with fruit of your choice!

Choco Taco

SERVINGS: 12

A taco cookbook wouldn't be complete without a recipe for a Choco Taco. This one requires a waffle maker and a little effort, but you'll love the results! There's nothing better than waffles topped with ice cream and chocolate!

½ cup white whole wheat flour

¼ teaspoon kosher salt

¼ cup powdered sugar, lightly scooped, sifted

1½ tablespoons melted butter (or vegetable oil)

1 large egg

¼ cup milk

¼ teaspoon pure vanilla extract

1 ¼ cup vanilla ice cream or frozen yogurt

2 ounces dark chocolate, melted

To get ready:

Wrap a cardboard paper towel roll (or the cardboard roll of foil or plastic wrap) in foil. Tear another sheet of foil as long as the roll.

To make the waffles:

Preheat the waffle maker. In a medium bowl, whisk together the flour and salt. In a separate large bowl, whisk together the sugar and butter until light yellow and frothy, about 1 to 2 minutes. Whisk in the egg, then the milk and vanilla extract. Add the flour mixture and stir until there are no longer any lumps.

Pour batter onto preheated waffle iron, just enough to reach the top of the waffle "nubbins," and spread out into a thin layer using an offset spatula or knife. (If using a round waffle maker, you'll need about 1 rounded tablespoon of batter for each 3-inch waffle) Cook until lightly browned (time varies upon model of waffle iron being used). Remove carefully from the waffle maker and lay over the foil-wrapped roll. Cover with the sheet of foil and wrap over the waffles to "bend" them into a taco. Let sit 1 to 2 minutes, remove the foil and taco shells from the roll. Set them aside to cool, then repeat with remaining batter.

To serve:

Fill "tacos" with ice cream, then top with a drizzle or dip of melted chocolate.

RECIPE NOTE: Waffles can also be made into taco shells by folding freshly cooked waffles and nestling them between the cups of an upside-down muffin tin.

Berry Tacos with Whipped Cream and Candied Pistachios

SERVINGS: 10

Did I just say, "Candied pistachios?" Yes, I sure did! And they make the perfect topping for these sweet berry tacos! They're so good, in fact, that you'll want to double the batch.

2 teaspoons light brown sugar

⅛ teaspoon kosher salt

1 teaspoon water

⅓ cup shelled pistachios

1 recipe Sweet Crepes
(see page 221)

2 cups berries (any mixture,
slice bigger berries)

¼ cup whipped cream

To make the candied pistachios:

Roughly chop the pistachios. Place the brown sugar, salt, and water in a non-stick skillet. Mix together and cook over medium-high heat until bubbly. Add the pistachios and cook 3 minutes, stirring often. Carefully remove the pistachios from the pan and transfer to a wire rack lined with parchment paper (or foil that's been coated in nonstick cooking spray) to cool.

To make the crepes:

Prepare according to recipe on page 221.

To assemble:

Portion berries among crepe taco shells. Top with a dollop of whipped cream and garnish with candied pistachios.

Brown Sugar Banana Crepe Tacos

SERVINGS: 5

Caramelized bananas get topped with peanuts, whipped cream, and chocolate shavings. Sounds pretty good, right?

½ recipe for Sweet Crepes (see page 221)

5 medium ripe bananas, cut into ½-inch slices

2 tablespoons salted butter

2 tablespoons packed light brown sugar

¼ cup chopped peanuts

¼ cup whipped cream

¼ cup dark chocolate shavings or mini chocolate chips

To make the crepes:

Prepare according to recipe on page 221 and keep them warm in a 300°F oven.

To make the bananas:

Set a large non-stick skillet over medium-high heat and add the butter. Once the butter has melted, add the banana slices. Cook 2 minutes on each side, adjusting heat to prevent any burning, then add the brown sugar to the pan, take off the heat, and gently toss with a wooden spoon to coat.

To serve the tacos:

Portion banana mixture evenly between the crepes. Top with peanuts, whipped cream, and chocolate shavings.

PREP TIP: Use a vegetable peeler to make chocolate shavings. It's easiest to do when you buy a bar of dark chocolate.

Cinnamon Sugar Tacos with Whipped Cream

SERVINGS: 12

What could be better than a sweet crepe "tortilla" filled with whipped cream? Nothing! Well, how about a crepe brushed with butter and topped with a sprinkle of cinnamon and sugar!

1 recipe Sweet Crepes
(see page 221)

1 teaspoon ground cinnamon

1 tablespoon granulated sugar

2 tablespoons salted butter, melted

Toppings: whipped cream, chocolate chips, sprinkles

To make the tortillas:

Prepare the Sweet Crepes according to recipe on page 221.

To make the churros:

Mix the cinnamon and sugar together in a small bowl.

Brush the inside of the freshly cooked crepes with a little butter, then sprinkle with the cinnamon sugar mixture. Fill with a little whipped cream and top with chocolate chips or sprinkles. Fold up like a taco and enjoy!

Key Lime Pie Tacos

SERVINGS: 10

Florida is one of my favorite places to vacation. And when I'm there, I always feel compelled to get a slice of key lime pie and it's ALWAYS so good. And I'm happy to tell you, it can be a pretty delicious dessert taco, too!

1 recipe Graham Cracker
Pancakes (see page 194)

To make the filling:

½ cup sweetened condensed
milk

¼ cup fresh lime juice

1 teaspoon lime zest + extra for
garnish

1 cup whipped cream

1 teaspoon powdered sugar

For the taco garnish:

¼ cup whipped cream

To make the pancakes:

Prepare the pancakes according to the recipe on
page 194.

To make the filling:

In a large bowl, whisk together the sweetened condensed
milk, lime juice, zest, and powdered sugar. Using a
spatula, carefully fold in the whipped cream. Refrigerate
until ready to use.

For assembling:

Once pancakes are cool, top with lime filling, a dollop
of whipped cream, and garnish with extra zest.

PREP TIP: You can make the filling about 1 day ahead
of time. Store in a sealed container in the refrigerator.

S'mores Tacos

SERVINGS: 12

Have s'mores night every night! All you need is to turn them into tacos! This recipe uses homemade graham cracker pancakes that get topped with chocolate and marshmallows and then get a quick broil in the oven. The result: ooey, gooey goodness!

For the graham cracker pancakes:

½ cup white whole wheat flour

1 ¼ cup graham cracker crumbs

½ teaspoon baking powder

¼ teaspoon baking soda

⅛ teaspoon salt

1 large egg

1 cup milk

1 tablespoon vegetable or canola oil

1 teaspoon pure vanilla extract

2 tablespoons packed light brown sugar

For the tacos:

1 cup mini chocolate chips

1 cup mini marshmallows

Kosher salt

To make the graham cracker pancakes:

In a large mixing bowl, whisk together the flour, graham cracker crumbs, baking powder, baking soda, and salt.

In a separate mixing bowl, whisk together the egg, milk, oil, vanilla, and brown sugar. Add dry mixture to wet mixture and stir gently until combined.

To cook the graham cracker pancakes:

Heat non-stick pan or griddle over medium-high heat. Once hot, spray with non-stick cooking spray and drop pancakes onto hot pan using a ⅛ measuring cup. Spread out into a 4-inch circle. Cook on the first side until batter begins to bubble, then flip and cook the other side an additional 2 to 3 minutes, or until lightly browned.

To make the tacos:

Place pancakes on a baking sheet and top each with a few mini chocolate chips, a few mini marshmallows, and a dash of salt. Broil for 1 minute, or until marshmallows are toasted. Sprinkle with a tiny pinch of salt, if desired, then fold up and serve.

RECIPE NOTE: Any type of milk would work fine here, even milk alternatives such as soy or almond milk.

Strawberry Angel Food Cake Tacos

SERVINGS: 12

Angel food cake topped with sliced strawberries is a dessert of my childhood. I love the pairing so much and wanted to create a taco to replicate it. And it's pretty easy to do! Just thinly slice the angel food cake, then top with sliced berries a bit of whipped cream.

12 strawberries, cored, then halved and sliced

¼ teaspoon granulated sugar

½ teaspoon lemon juice

Angel food cake, prepared (or jelly roll cake), cut into 12 ½-inch slices

¾ cup whipped cream

To prepare the berries:

Place the sliced berries in a medium bowl and toss with sugar and lemon juice. Set aside.

To prepare the cake taco shells:

Using a rolling pin, roll slices of cake into 3½ x 2-inch rectangles, ¼-inch thick.

To make the tacos:

Place berries among angel food slices, then top with whipped cream.

GROCERY TIP: If you can't find angel food cake, feel free to swap in pound cake. This swap will make this dessert a bit heavier.

COOKING TIP: If you're feeling fancy, whisk in about ½ teaspoon of pure vanilla extract into the whipped cream.

Cherry Almond Cheesecake Tacos

SERVINGS: 5

My grandmother was famous for her cherry pie. It wasn't traditional—she used almonds and almond extract for a fun twist, and it was fabulous. She was a great cook and I loved her food, and these little Cherry Almond Cheesecake Tacos are in honor of her!

For the filling:

½ cup heavy whipping cream, very cold

4 ounces Neufchâtel cheese

¼ cup powdered sugar

½ recipe Graham Cracker Pancakes (see page 194)

For the topping:

1 cup frozen sweet cherries, thawed, solids and liquids

½ cup crumbled graham crackers

¼ cup sliced almonds, toasted

To make the filling:

Place the cream in a large bowl and, using a hand mixer or whisk, whip until soft peaks form.

In a separate large bowl, whip the Neufchâtel cheese with the sugar. Carefully stir in whipped cream. Spoon the mixture into a pie pan or other shallow dish, cover and chill in fridge for at least 2 hours.

While mixture is cooling, make the Graham Cracker Pancakes:

Prepare according to recipe on page 194.

To serve the tacos:

Spoon whipped cream mixture into graham pancakes. Top with thawed cherries and juice, crumbled graham crackers, and almonds.

RECIPE NOTE: You could use full fat cream cheese, too, but to lighten it up here, I've used its lower-fat counterpart, Neufchâtel cheese.

Apple Pie Tacos

SERVINGS: 12

You don't have to mess with a pie shell for this apple pie. Instead, use frozen puff pastry and a muffin pan! You'll get a delicious hand-held taco-esque apple pie!

For the puff pastry taco shells:

½ sheet puff pastry, thawed

For the apple filling:

2 to 3 medium apples, peeled and diced small (Granny Smith, Jonagold, Golden Delicious are good options)

1 teaspoon ground cinnamon

Pinch kosher salt

⅛ teaspoon ground nutmeg

¼ cup granulated sugar

1 teaspoon cornstarch

1 teaspoon lemon juice

½ teaspoon pure vanilla extract

For the tacos:

Whipped cream

Ground cinnamon

Preheat the oven to 400°F. Spray the cups of a 12-cup muffin pan generously with non-stick cooking spray. Set aside.

To make the puff pastry tacos:

Dust a clean work surface with flour. Carefully roll puff pastry out into a 12-inch square. Cut into 12 rectangular pieces, about 4 by 3 inches each. Press rectangles into muffin cups. Set aside.

To make the apple filling:

In a small saucepan, combine the apples, cinnamon, salt, nutmeg, and sugar and set over medium heat. Cook 10 minutes, stirring often. In a small bowl, mix the corn starch with 1 tablespoon water. Add to the apple filling and cook an additional minute. Stir in the lemon juice and vanilla extract.

Divide apple mixture among muffin cups. Bake for 22 to 25 minutes, until golden. Cool in pan for 5 minutes, then carefully remove to a wire rack.

To make the tacos:

Garnish with whipped cream and a sprinkle of cinnamon for serving.

PREP TIP: Puff pastry can be thawed overnight in the refrigerator.

COOKING TIP: A pizza cutter works great for slicing the puff pastry into rectangular pieces.

KID'S RECIPES

Because I know kids like tacos too, I've enlisted the help of some very special kids to help with recipes in this section of the book! You'll see plenty of great ideas here, all of which have been "kid approved!"

Little Sous Chef's Hummus Tacos

SERVINGS: 4

My daughter has loved hummus since she was little, so it only made sense for her to make a taco using one of her favorite foods. You can make your own hummus for this or buy it pre-made to make life a little easier!

For the hummus:

1 (15-ounce can) chickpeas, drained and rinsed

1 tablespoon tahini

2 tablespoons extra-virgin olive oil

1 tablespoon + 2 teaspoons lemon juice

¼ teaspoon kosher salt

½ teaspoon lemon zest

For the tacos shells:

4 (6-inch) flour tortillas or yogurt flatbreads (see page 230), warmed

For the topping:

Shredded or thinly sliced carrot

Shredded lettuce or cabbage

1 cucumber, thinly sliced into rounds

To make the hummus:

Place the chickpeas in the bowl of a food processor along with the tahini, olive oil, lemon juice, and salt. Puree until smooth, scraping down the sides of the bowl occasionally. Remove and place in a bowl. Stir in the lemon zest.

To serve the tacos:

If desired, use round cookie cutters to make smaller tortilla rounds. Spread hummus onto mini tortilla rounds and top with shredded carrots, lettuce, and cucumber. Optional: have kids use small cookie cutter shapes to cut cucumber slices into fun pieces.

SAVING TIP: Got extra hummus? Place it in a sealed container in the refrigerator and use within two to three days.

Noah's Sweet Potato, Black Bean and Chicken Tacos

SERVINGS: 4

This recipe is proof that kids like fun, nourishing foods! Can you believe that this is what the little sous chef's friend helps his mom make in the kitchen?

1 large sweet potato, cleaned

1 (15-ounce) can no-salt-added black beans, drained and rinsed

2 boneless, skinless chicken breasts or 8 ounces cooked chicken

¼ teaspoon kosher salt

⅛ teaspoon freshly cracked black pepper

1 tablespoon plain Greek yogurt

6 ounces white cheddar cheese, shredded

4 (6-inch) corn tortillas, warmed

1 ripe avocado or guacamole for garnish/dipping

Preheat the grill to medium-high heat or set a grill pan over medium-high heat. If using the grill, clean the grill grates and brush them with oil. If using a grill pan, coat pan lightly with oil.

To make the sweet potato:

Preheat the oven to 350°F. Prick the sweet potato all over with a fork, then place it on a baking sheet and bake for 35 minutes, or until soft. (Alternatively, set the potato on a microwave-safe plate and microwave for 5 minutes, flipping once halfway through cooking time.)

To prepare the black beans:

Add the beans to a sauce pan set over low heat. Stir in the garlic powder along with the salt. Turn heat to low and stir occasionally, cooking until warmed, about 10 minutes.

To cook the chicken:

Season the chicken breast with salt and pepper. Place the chicken on the grill and cook about 5 to 7 minutes per side, or until internal temperature reaches 165°F. Let the chicken rest for 5 minutes.

While the chicken is cooking, prepare the potato:

Scoop the flesh out of the sweet potato into a small bowl, add the yogurt, and season lightly with salt and pepper. Smash to combine.

. . . continued on next page

To make the tacos:

Thinly slice or chop the chicken. Spread the sweet potato onto the tortillas then layer with black beans, chicken, and shredded cheese. Top with diced avocado or guacamole.

RECIPE NOTE: To make this vegetarian, just skip the chicken!

SERVING TIP: For a quick weeknight meal, Noah's mom suggests serving this taco as a quesadilla with store-bought individual guacamole cups for dipping.

Madeleine's Mexican Tacos

SERVINGS: 5

For the chicken:

1½ pounds boneless, skinless chicken breast

1 cup low-sodium chicken broth

1 tablespoon chili powder

1 teaspoon ground cumin

3 cloves of garlic

½ teaspoon kosher salt

For the guacamole:

2 large, ripe avocados

½ teaspoon of onion powder

¼ teaspoon ground cumin

1 tablespoon fresh lime juice

1 large tomato, seeded and diced small

For the lime dressing:

½ cup extra-virgin olive oil

¼ teaspoon kosher salt

1 lime, juiced

¼ teaspoon garlic, finely minced

For the tacos:

10 hard taco shells, (or you can use soft shells if you prefer)

Toppings: cilantro, diced bell peppers, cooked corn, black beans, sour cream or plain Greek yogurt

My niece is an AWESOME cook! I mean, check out this recipe she made! And I love her thoughts on it too, "I like using fresh herbs from our garden in the summer. My family loves my recipe because it is healthy and delicious!" Indeed!

To prepare the chicken:

Place chicken in a crock-pot along with the broth, chili powder, cumin, garlic, and salt. Cook on high for about 4 hours. Once cooked, remove the chicken and shred using two forks. Return chicken back to crock pot and move setting to "warm."

To make the guacamole:

Slice avocados in half and remove the seed. Scoop out the flesh and add to a medium bowl. Mash the avocado with a fork then stir in the onion powder, cumin, and lime juice. Season to taste with salt, then gently mix in the tomatoes.

To make the dressing:

Combine oil, salt, lime juice, and garlic in a bowl and whisk.

To make the tacos:

Serve chicken in warmed taco shells; add any of your favorite toppings, then top with guacamole and lime dressing.

RECIPE NOTE: If you don't have a lime, you can use 1 to 2 tablespoons of apple cider vinegar.

Makena's Fruit Tacos

SERVINGS: 1

Fruit tacos are where it's at! And the little sous chef's friend has created a pretty delicious one. These fruit tacos are perfect for little hands to make and eat!

1 flour tortilla

1 tablespoon whipped berry cream cheese

5 to 8 blueberries

1 to 2 strawberries, stemmed and sliced

4 to 5 grapes, halved

Lay the tortilla on a plate or clean work surface. Spread cream cheese down the middle of the tortilla. Top with blueberries, strawberries, and grapes. Fold up and enjoy.

RECIPE NOTE: You can substitute your favorite fruits here, too.

COOKING TIP: Don't have berry cream cheese? You can make your own! I like to use 4 ounces Neufchâtel cheese and beat it at high speed with ½ cup chopped fresh strawberries or other fruit. Use immediately or refrigerate up to four days.

Teagan I.'s Summer Corn and Bean Tacos

SERVINGS: 4

Even kids like vegetarian options! These tacos were a creation by another one of my lovely nieces! Teagan is super handy in the kitchen and I love that she added a hit of heat to her recipe!

For the taco sauce:

1 tablespoon Sriracha

¼ cup olive oil mayonnaise

1 teaspoon fresh lime juice

For the taco filling:

3 ears of corn, husked, silks removed

2 teaspoons vegetable oil

2 large, ripe tomatoes, diced

1 (15-ounce) can black beans, drained, rinsed and warmed

2 teaspoons fresh lime juice

kosher salt and black pepper

For the tacos:

8 hard shell tacos, warmed

1 cup shredded Colby jack cheese

2 cups shredded lettuce or cabbage

To make the taco sauce:

In a small bowl, combine the Sriracha, mayonnaise and lime juice. Set aside.

To make the taco filling:

Preheat the grill to high heat or set a grill pan over medium-high heat. (If using a grill, clean the grill grates and brush them with additional oil. If using a grill pan, coat pan lightly with oil.) Brush corn all over with the 2 teaspoons of oil. Grill the corn, turning often, until browned and heated through, about 10 minutes. Transfer to a plate and allow to cool slightly. Once cool to the touch, cut kernels from cobs and place in a medium bowl. Add the tomatoes, beans and lime juice and toss to combine. Season to taste with salt and pepper.

To make the tacos:

Serve bean mixture in warmed taco shells with taco sauce, cheese and lettuce.

COOKING TIP: If you don't have a grill, use a cast-iron pan or other heavy skillet to cook the corn. Set the pan over medium-high heat and use the same method of oiling and turning often.

SERVING TIP: If you prefer, omit taco sauce and substitute with salsa of your choice or even guacamole!

TORTILLAS AND OTHER GOOD STUFF

This book is all about tacos, but I figured you might want some other tasty recipes too. How about some homemade tortillas? They're easier to make then you might think! And what about salsa, guacamole and pickled onions? Don't worry, they're in this section too!

Homemade Flour Tortillas

MAKES: 12 (6-INCH) TORTILLAS

Making homemade tortillas is EASY! And I promise you that they taste so much better than most store-bought versions. This one can easily be made 100% whole grain by swapping out the all-purpose flour for white whole wheat flour.

1 cup white whole wheat flour

1 cup all-purpose flour

½ teaspoon kosher salt

1 teaspoon baking powder

2 tablespoons lard (or other fat, see tip below)

⅔ cup warm water (plus more, if needed)

To make the dough:

In a large bowl, mix together the flours, salt and baking powder. Work in fat using clean fingers or the back of a fork. Add liquid all at once and work into dough using your hands or fork. Add more liquid, 1 tablespoon at a time, if dough seems too dry. Knead the dough until a smooth ball forms, about 4 to 5 minutes. Dough should be tacky (moist, but not wet). Set aside, cover with plastic wrap or towel, and rest 10 minutes.

To make the tortillas:

Divide dough into 12 equal pieces and shape into balls. On a lightly floured surface, roll out each dough ball into a thin 6-inch round.

To cook the tortillas:

Set a heavy non-stick skillet, such as cast-iron, over medium heat. Once hot, add the tortillas, one at a time, and cook 30 seconds per side. Wrap cooked tortillas in tea towel to keep moist and warm.

PREP TIP: No one's perfect! That means your tortillas won't be, either. Don't fret if they aren't perfect circles. But if you are an over-achiever, take a hint from professional bakers and use that rolling pin to your advantage. Instead of using a back-and-forth motion, roll once in one direction, and then give the tortilla a ¼ turn. Repeat the process until you get a circle, or something that resembles a circle.

. . . continued on next page

RECIPE NOTE: You can easily make this a 100% whole wheat tortilla. Just use 2 cups white whole wheat flour and omit the all-purpose flour.

RECIPE NOTE: The choice of fat is up to you! You can use lard, butter, or oil. Just about any fat will work here.

KITCHEN TIP: If you have a tortilla press, use it! Just follow the instructions that came with it on the best method for using it!

SAVING TIP: Have extra tortillas? Layer cooled tortillas between pieces of parchment paper and then place them in a sealable freezer bag. Freeze for up to six months.

Savory Crepes

MAKES: 10 CREPES

I may not call for these savory crepes too often, but they make for a unique twist on any of these taco recipes. Try them out, you'll love them.

4 ounces eggs (about 2 large)

½ cup + 1 tablespoon milk

1 ounce all-purpose flour (about ¼ cup)

1 ounce white whole wheat flour (about ¼ cup)

⅛ teaspoon kosher salt

2 tablespoons melted, unsalted butter

To make the crepe batter:

Place all ingredients in a blender and blend until smooth, about 10 to 12 seconds. Let rest 30 minutes.

To cook the crepes:

Set an 8-inch non-stick pan over medium-low heat. Brush pan with butter, then pour 1 ounce (⅛ cup) of the batter into the pan, swirl the batter to coat pan. Cook 45 seconds. Carefully loosen crepe from pan, flip, and cook an additional 20 seconds. Remove from pan and keep warm. Repeat with the remaining batter. Place a piece of parchment or wax paper between each crepe to preventing sticking.

RECIPE NOTE: You don't need a crepe pan to make these. Your 8-inch non-stick skillet will be just fine to handle the job.

SAVING TIP: Have extra crepes? Layer cooled crepes between pieces of parchment paper and then place them in a sealable freezer bag. Freeze for up to one month.

Homemade Corn Tortillas

MAKES: 12 (6-INCH) TORTILLAS

Have you ever had a fresh, homemade corn tortilla? Um, they're AMAZING! You'll love how easy these tortillas are to make, too! If you have a tortilla press, I definitely recommend you use it for these. It just makes the job even easier!

1 ¾ cups masa harina

½ teaspoon kosher salt

1 cup + 2 tablespoons warm water

To make the dough:

In a large bowl, mix masa harina and salt. Add the warm water and mix dough with a fork. Once combined, knead with clean hands for about 1 minute and shape into a ball. If dough feels overly dry and crumbly, add water, 1 tablespoon at a time, until dough can easily be gathered up in a ball without breaking apart. If dough feels wet, add more masa harina, 1 tablespoon at a time. Cover bowl with a clean towel or plastic wrap and let rest for 10 minutes.

To make the tortillas:

Divide dough into 12 equal pieces and shape into balls. Lightly dust a clean work surface with some of the masa, then roll out each dough ball into a thin, 6-inch round.

To cook the tortillas:

Set a heavy non-stick skillet, such as cast-iron, over medium heat. Once hot, add the tortillas, one or two at a time, and cook, 1 minute per side, or until dry and brown spots appear. Wrap cooked tortillas in a clean tea towel to keep moist and warm.

GROCERY TIP: You can usually find masa harina located near the other Mexican food at the grocery store. If your store doesn't carry it, try a Mexican grocery store or order online.

. . . continued on next page

PREP TIP: No one's perfect! That means your tortillas won't be either. Don't fret if they aren't perfect circles. But if you are an over-achiever, take a hint from professional bakers and use that rolling pin to your advantage. Instead of using a back-and-forth motion, roll once in one direction, and then give the tortilla a ¼ turn. Repeat the process until you get a circle, or something that resembles a circle.

KITCHEN TIP: You'll likely have to buy a large bag of masa harina (because that's how it's usually sold). Have no fear! You can use it to make the Turn Up Da Beet Falafel Tacos (see page 139). It's also great for making tamales or empanada dough. And if you need to thicken up a hearty soup or stew, use some of that masa harina.

INGREDIENT TIP: Masa harina is created by soaking and softening corn kernels in a lime water solution. The kernels are then ground into dough (masa). The dough is then dried and turned into flour known as "masa harina."

SAVING TIP: Have extra tortillas? Layer cooled tortillas between pieces of parchment paper and then place them in a sealable freezer bag. Freeze for up to six months.

Sweet Crepes

MAKES: 10 CREPES

Crepes make the perfect tortillas! Especially for desserts. You'll find that I use these a lot in the dessert taco recipes. And for good reason—they taste good and are pliable. That makes them perfect for holding delicious fruits and whipped cream!

4 ounces eggs (about 2 large)

½ cup + 1 tablespoon milk

1 ounce all-purpose flour (about ¼ cup)

1 ounce white whole wheat flour (about ¼ cup)

1½ teaspoons granulated sugar

⅛ teaspoon kosher salt

2 tablespoons melted, unsalted butter + extra for cooking

To make the crepe batter:

Place all ingredients in a blender and blend until smooth, about 10 to 12 seconds. Let rest 30 minutes.

To cook the crepes:

Set an 8-inch non-stick pan over medium-low heat. Brush pan with butter, then pour 1 ounce (⅛ cup) of the batter into the pan, swirl the batter to coat pan. Cook 45 seconds. Carefully loosen crepe from pan, flip, and cook an additional 20 seconds. Remove from pan and keep warm. Repeat with the remaining batter. Place a piece of parchment or wax paper between each crepe to prevent sticking.

RECIPE NOTE: You don't need a crepe pan to make these. Your 8-inch non-stick skillet will be just fine to handle the job.

SAVING TIP: Have extra crepes? Layer cooled crepes between pieces of parchment paper and then place them in a sealable freezer bag. Freeze for up to one month.

Jalapeño Honeydew Salsa

MAKES: 1½ CUPS SALSA

I love unique salsas, especially ones that call for fruit. This one is refreshing and spicy! It's the perfect pairing for fish tacos or as a delightful appetizer for a hot day.

½ cup diced honeydew melon

1 tablespoon red onion, finely chopped

1 tablespoon jalapeño, finely chopped (for spicier version, keep membranes and seeds)

1 teaspoon fresh lime zest

1 tablespoon fresh lime juice

1 tablespoon fresh cilantro, chopped

⅛ teaspoon kosher salt

Combine all ingredients in a large bowl and mix well to combine. Add additional lime juice or zest to taste. Serve immediately or refrigerate.

RECIPE NOTE: If you can't find a good honeydew melon, you could also use cantaloupe or seedless watermelon for this recipe.

SERVING TIP: Serve with tortilla chips or use as a topper for fish tacos. This salsa also tastes great on ice cream or plain Greek yogurt!

Creamy Cilantro Dressing

MAKES: 6 FLUID OUNCES

A salad is always a great accompaniment to any taco meal! And this salad dressing is a lovely way to "dress" it!

¼ cup plain Greek yogurt

¼ cup extra-virgin olive oil mayonnaise

½ cup cilantro, leaves and stems

1 clove garlic

1 tablespoon fresh lime juice

Kosher salt and freshly ground black pepper

Place all the ingredients in a blender or small food processor and blend until smooth. Season with salt and pepper to taste.

Alternatively, place all of the ingredients in a mixing bowl (be sure to finely chop the cilantro first) and whisk together.

SAVING TIP: Store dressing in an air-tight container for up to three days in the refrigerator.

Pickled Red Onions

MAKES: ABOUT 2 CUPS

I super LOVE pickled red onions. They make me incredibly happy. They are a lovely accompaniment to many of the tacos in this book. And if you want to spice them up, add a few slices of jalapeño pepper to the mix.

1 medium red onion

4 cups water

2 sprigs fresh thyme (or 1 teaspoon dried thyme leaves)

½ cup white distilled vinegar

¼ cup white wine vinegar

¼ cup orange juice

½ teaspoon coriander seeds

8 black peppercorns

½ teaspoon kosher salt

Slice onion into ¼-inch thick slices and then place them into a medium, non-reactive bowl (such as glass or stainless steel). Place the water in a small pot and cook over high heat until boiling. Once boiling, pour over onions. Let sit about 15 seconds, then strain the onions in a colander or strainer set over the sink. Once drained, transfer the onions back to the non-reactive bowl, add the thyme, and set aside.

To the now dry pot, add distilled vinegar, white wine vinegar, orange juice, coriander seeds, black peppercorns, and salt. Set over medium heat and allow it to come to just a boil, about 5 to 6 minutes. Remove from the heat and pour over the onions. Stir, then pack mixture down with a spoon. Allow to cool about 20 to 30 minutes, pack down again, cover, and refrigerate. Let "pickle" in the fridge for at least 2 hours.

RECIPE NOTE: You can replace the white wine vinegar with other vinegars, such as red wine vinegar or apple cider vinegar. The white vinegar can also be replaced with lemon or lime juice!

Homemade Refried Pinto Beans

MAKES: ABOUT 5 CUPS

Why would you make homemade refined beans? My answer would be, "Why wouldn't you make homemade refried beans?" You already know this, because I've said it a million times, but homemade always tastes better!

1 pound dry pinto beans, picked over, rinsed and soaked overnight

2 cloves garlic, smashed

1 small white onion, chopped

¼ teaspoon kosher salt, plus more to taste

3 tablespoons vegetable oil

1 teaspoon dried oregano

To cook the beans:

Place soaked beans in a large pot, along with the garlic and onion. Cover with water by 2 inches and set over high heat. Bring beans to a boil, reduce heat, and simmer, partially covered, for 1 to 1½ hours. Add salt 20 minutes before the end of cooking time.

To make the refried beans:

Working in batches, heat oil 1 tablespoon at a time in a large skillet (cast iron works best) over medium-high heat, add ⅓ of the bean mixture (liquid and beans) and cook, stirring often, in the oil for about 3 minutes. Add the beans to a mixing bowl. Repeat with remaining oil and beans. Once all the beans are cooked, mash them with a potato or avocado masher until you reach the desired consistency. Add the oregano and season to taste with additional salt.

COOKING TIP: These beans are a blank canvas, so feel free to add your favorite flavors here, too! Jalapeños, ground cumin, cilantro, cheese, and other additions only make these beans more fabulous!

COOKING TIP: If you don't have a potato or avocado masher, you could also use a fork or a pastry cutter to smash the beans.

Super Simple Homemade Guacamole

SERVINGS: 4

Guacamole is my obsession. And I like to keep it simple. That means no tomatoes or other "add-ins" for me. The key to a good guacamole? Fresh lime juice and the right amount of salt!

1 large, ripe avocado

2 tablespoons minced white onion

½ jalapeño, finely minced

1 tablespoon fresh lime juice

¼ teaspoon kosher salt

¼ cup lightly packed cilantro, roughly chopped

Scoop out the avocado and place in a medium bowl. Mash with the back of a fork, then add the onion, jalapeño, lime juice, salt, and cilantro. Stir to combine. Enjoy immediately.

COOKING TIP: If you like things spicy, don't remove the membranes or seeds before chopping the jalapeño!

SERVING TIP: I love this guacamole served with tortilla chips, but it's also a fabulous dip for veggies!

Yogurt Flatbreads

SERVINGS: 6

I love the tang of Greek yogurt. And it's delicious in these flatbreads. These are a great base for tacos too! And guess what, no yeast or heavy mixing is needed to make them! Yahoo!

1 cup white whole wheat flour

¼ teaspoon kosher salt

½ cup + 2 tablespoons plain, whole fat Greek yogurt

1 teaspoon dried herbs, if desired

To make the dough:

In a medium bowl, combine the flour and salt. Using a spoon, mix in the yogurt. Once dough starts to come together, use your hands and knead into a ball in the bowl. Knead for a few minutes. Then cover with plastic wrap and let dough rest 5 minutes.

To shape the flatbread:

Divide dough into pieces of equal size and shape into balls. Dust work surface with flour and roll each piece out into a 5-inch diameter circle. Use additional flour as needed to prevent dough from sticking to work surface.

To cook the flatbread:

Heat a heavy non-stick pan, such as a cast iron pan, over medium-high heat. Coat with a little bit of vegetable oil, then add 1 of the flatbreads. Cook 1 minute, flip with tongs, then cook an additional minute. Transfer to a clean towel and cover to keep warm while you cook the remaining flatbreads.

COOKING TIP: Boost flavor by adding garlic! Finely mince 1 clove of garlic, then sauté it in 1 tablespoon butter for 1 to 2 minutes in small sauté pan set over medium heat. Add garlic and butter to the dough mixture and prepare as above.

SAVING TIP: Have extra flatbreads? Layer cooled flatbreads between pieces of parchment paper and then place them in a sealable freezer bag. Freeze for up to six months.

Tortillas de Azucar

MAKES: 12 TORTILLAS

Heads-up! This is a bonus tortilla recipe! Consider it more of a snack or dessert tortilla. Perfect paired with a cup of coffee or tea!

1 cup white whole wheat flour

3 tablespoons granulated sugar

½ teaspoon kosher salt

¼ cup fat*

½ large egg

2 tablespoons warm milk (plus more, if needed)

To make the dough:

In a large bowl, mix together the flour, sugar and salt. Work in fat using clean fingers or a fork, until dough is crumbly, resembling sand. Add the egg and milk and mix to combine using your hands or other clean utensil. Add in more milk, 1 tablespoon at a time, if dough is too dry. Knead until smooth ball forms, about 4 to 5 minutes. Dough should be tacky (moist, but not wet). Rest 10 minutes.

To make the tortillas:

Divide the dough into 12 equal pieces, about 1 tablespoon each. Roll out each piece into a thin circle, about ⅛-inch thick.

To cook the tortillas:

Set a heavy non-stick skillet, such as cast-iron, over medium heat. Once hot, add the tortillas, one at a time, and cook, about 30 to 45 seconds per side. Wrap cooked tortillas in tea to towel to keep moist and warm. Or enjoy right away!

PREP TIP: Did I really call for half of an egg in the recipe? I did, how annoying of me, I know, but that's really all you need. You can save the other half and use it the next time you make scrambled eggs. The easiest way to measure half an egg is to crack it in a bowl and remove 1½ tablespoons—that's about half of an egg.

RECIPE NOTE: Any type of fat here works well. I like the flavor of coconut oil for these slightly sweetened tortillas!

SAVING TIP: Have extra tortillas? Layer cooled tortillas between pieces of parchment paper and then place them in a sealable freezer bag. Freeze for up to six months.

Acknowledgements

Many, many thanks to:

My family: Michael and my little sous chef, my mom and dad and all of my other amazingly supportive family members. And a big thank you to my uncle, Richard Reed, for reviewing this book. No one knows the English language like you do, Uncle Rick! You're my Superman!

My friends: My dear friend Elizabeth Shaw and all of the other fabulous friends who have provided encouragement and support throughout the years!

My recipe testers: A huge, big thank you to all of the fabulous people who helped test the recipes for this book! I couldn't have done it without you! Patty Duff and family, your help was priceless!

A special thanks KJ Pottery (www.kjpottery.com); her beautiful pottery appears in the photos throughout this book, and I absolutely love them.

About the Author

A FOOD AND NUTRITION EXPERT with formal training in culinary arts, Sara has been a registered and licensed dietitian since 2002 and a professional chef since 2008.

She is an author of *The Fertility Foods Cookbook* and is a past National Academy of Nutrition and Dietetics Media Spokesperson, lending her talents to all forms of media, and has been featured in *Shape Magazine*, USA Today, *The Wall Street Journal*, *The Huffington Post*, Epicurious.com, BabyCenter.com, *Glamour Magazine*, *O Magazine* and *Today's Dietitian Magazine*.

Sara is a contributing writer for *Eating Well Magazine* as well as *Food and Nutrition Magazine* and writes for its Stone Soup Blog. She is a feed editor for the FeedFeed and has created recipes for organizations including Kids Eat Right and The Hass Avocado Board. Sara also shares her love of food and nutrition on her website, www.sarahaasrdn.com, where she posts recipes and nutrition-related blog posts.

Sara graduated from Indiana University with a Bachelor of Science degree in Nutrition and Dietetics, completed her dietetic internship at the University of Massachusetts and earned her associates degree in culinary arts at the Cooking and Hospitality Institute of Chicago, Le Cordon Bleu Program. She is a member of the Academy of Nutrition and Dietetics, the Chicago Academy of Nutrition and Dietetics, the Food and Culinary Professionals Dietetic Practice Group and she is also a member of the Nutrition Entrepreneurs Dietetics Practice Group where she served on the Executive Committee as Director of Awards and Networking.

Recipe Index

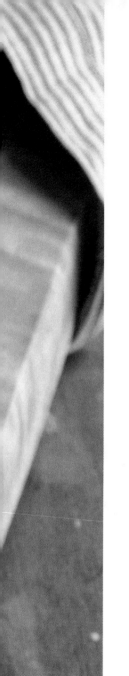